Profitability Through Loss Control

B. I. Ehrstine and J. A. Mack

ap since 1887
anderson publishing co./cincinnati

Library of Congress Catalog Card Number: 76-52634

ISBN 0-87084-719-8

Contents

Contributors

B.I. Ehrstine and J.A. Mack wish to acknowledge their debt to the many security professionals without whose contributions this publication would not have been possible. Certain material contained in "Profitability Through Loss Control" was extracted, in part, from published and unpublished matter provided by the following law enforcement and security professional organizations and persons:

Federal Bureau of Investigation

United States Secret Service

American Society for Industrial Security

American Bankers Association

Sam E. Bray
Director of Security
Continental Bank
Chicago, Ill. 60690

John B. Hitchins, retired
Sharon, Massachusetts

Harold W. Wallgren
Vice President & Cashier
Philadelphia Nat'l Bank
Philadelphia, Penn.

Gerard J. Kenna
President
Execudec, Inc.
Internal Security Specialists

Introduction

Loss Control

Loss Control encompasses many aspects of crime. As we become aware of the problems of financial institutions, we can better understand the enormity of the losses suffered annually, and hopefully, better prepare ourselves to defend against them.

Statistics gathered over the past few years show that losses due to stolen, forged and counterfeit checks have cost banks and merchants a minimum of one billion dollars a year, and an additional four and one-half billion dollars for investigation and prosecutions. Shop lifting (in banking circles we refer to them as sneak thefts) costs an estimated two billion dollars, and dishonest employees cost companies four to seven billion dollars per year.

To expand further on the topic of dishonest employees, according to United States Government statistics, 10% of your employees will not steal under any circumstances, and 80% will steal if given the opportunity. When dishonest employees are caught and given a polygraph test, it is found that 80% have stolen from a previous employer.

It is interesting to note that of the 1,500 businesses that go bankrupt each year, 30% is due to dishonest employees.

The noted National Conference on Crime Control in Washington, advises that white-collar crimes, including schemes for cheating the consumer, may pose a greater danger to national life than crimes of violence. Can we honestly look at ourselves and say we are not becoming a society of chiselers?

The Right to Steal?

At long last, our American society has developed beyond that archaic document called the Constitution and created another new and innovative right—we have the RIGHT to steal. Does a statement like this shock you? If so, it is apparent that the new trends in our society have developed while you remained hidden in your cocoon of complacency. A book written in 1967, called "Tally's Corner" by Dr. Elliot Liebow alludes to the fact (on page 37-38) that employees steal to compensate for low wages and some bankers plan on this thievery as part of the salary that does not have to be paid. It may even be considered as a bonus, for such losses can be written off for tax purposes. Liebow's book alludes to the fact that businessmen find this a cheap way to make money. As staggering as this concept appears, another author has expounded a similar theory in an article written for the June, 1971, issue of the magazine "Psychology Today." Dr. Lawrence R. Zeitlin, a noted psychologist, now a professor of industrial psychology at City College, City University of New York has gone so far as to say that "A little larceny can do a lot for employee morale."

Zeitlin's article continually refers to "acceptable levels" of stealing and indicated that this could be a solution to many businessmen's problems if they recognize that thievery, by their employees, is inevitable. An extension of this thought pattern into the area of banking and financial institutions could create an economic holocaust that would wreck our financial stability.

If this theory is taught and accepted, how is our society to cope with the fast growing problem of social justification that pilferage and stealing is an accepted way of life? Maybe it is time that we, as security specialists, intensify our efforts to teach courses to the youth of today to counter this malicious trend toward justified crime.

The associate editor of the Harvard Business Review, Mr. David W. Ewing, rejected Dr. Zeitlin's article on this subject. His rejection indicates that radical deviation such as expounded by Dr. Zeitlin is not acceptable to respectable business and certainly should not be accepted by the banking industry.

How long can we as bankers and American citizens tolerate a concept of stealing as a way of life? Now, TODAY, is the time to tackle the problem of stealing. Stop it now and our society of tomorrow will be a better one. All crime prevention techniques and programs are only tools of the "establishment" to assure that we have a safe community for tomorrow's citizens.

Another question we can ask is what does stealing cost us on an individual basis as a financial institution?

Most of our individual fraud or theft losses fall in a range from $20 to $300 each. From the following table you can quickly determine the value of loans or investments at various per annum percentage rates needed to offset a fraud or theft loss within the stipulated range.

AMOUNT OF LOSS

Per Annum Investment	$20	$50	$100	$150	$200	$250	$300
1.5%	1333	3333	6666	10000	13333	16666	20000
2%	1000	2500	5000	7500	10000	12500	15000
3%	666	1666	3333	5000	6666	8333	10000
4%	500	1250	2500	3750	5000	6250	7500
5%	400	1000	2000	3000	4000	5000	6000
6%	333	833	1666	2500	3333	4166	5000

Another indication of the cost of losses is a table based on a 1974 Federal Reserve functional cost report. It indicates the amount of each type of loan or deposit needed to produce annual earnings to offset a $100 loss due to theft or fraud.

Commercial Loan $2601
Mortgage Loan $6031
Installment Loan $3177
Demand Deposit Balance $2216
Savings Account Balance $5605
(Regular Passbook)

The Bank Protection Act

In 1968 Congress passed the Bank Protection Act, which was signed into law to become effective on January 13, 1969.

The Act applied to all financial institutions which were chartered by the federal government, or were members of the Federal Reserve System, or whose deposits were insured by either the Federal Deposit Insurance Corporation or the Federal Savings and Loan Insurance Corporation.

The Act set minimum standards for the protection of assets of these financial institutions, principally against robbery, burglary and larceny. Enforcement of these standards was the responsibility of the various federal controlling agencies.

1) The Comptroller of the Currency
2) The Federal Reserve System Board
3) The Federal Home Loan Board
4) The Federal Deposit Insurance Corporation

In 1973 the Act was amended to upgrade the minimum standards for security devices installed by financial institutions.

The following pages contain the Bank Protection Act, requirements, with amendments, as applicable to all federally controlled financial institutions.

BANK PROTECTION ACT OF 1968

Act of July 7, 1968 (82 Stat. 294)

To provide security measures for banks and other financial institutions, and to provide for the appointment of the Federal Savings and Loan Insurance Corporation as receiver.

Be it enacted by the Senate and House of Representatives of the United States of America in Congress assembled, That this Act may be cited as the "Bank Protection Act of 1968."

SEC. 2. As used in this Act the term "Federal supervisory agency" means—

(1) The Comptroller of the Currency with respect to national banks and district banks,

(2) The Board of Governors of the Federal Reserve System with respect to Federal Reserve banks and State banks which

are members of the Federal Reserve System,

(3) The Federal Deposit Insurance Corporation with respect to State banks which are not members of the Federal Reserve System but the deposits of which are insured by the Federal Deposit Insurance Corporation, and

(4) The Federal Home Loan Bank Board with respect to Federal savings and loan associations, and institutions the accounts of which are insured by the Federal Savings and Loan Insurance Corporation.

SEC. 3. (a) Within six months from the date of this Act, each Federal supervisory agency shall promulgate rules establishing minimum standards with which each bank or savings and loan association must comply with respect to the installation, maintenance, and operation of security devices and procedures, reasonable in cost, to discourage robberies, burglaries, and larcenies and to assist in the identification and apprehension of persons who commit such acts.

(b) The rules shall establish the time limits within which banks and savings and loan associations shall comply with the standards and shall require the submission of periodic reports with respect to the installation, maintenance, and operation of security devices and procedures.

SEC. 4. The Federal supervisory agencies shall consult with

(1) Insurers furnishing insurance protection against losses resulting from robberies, burglaries, and larcenies committed against financial institutions referred to in section 2, and

(2) State agencies having supervisory or regulatory responsibilities with respect to such insurers

to determine the feasibility and desirability of premium rate differentials based on the installation, maintenance, and operation of security devices and procedures. The Federal supervisory agencies shall report to the Congress the results of their consultations pursuant to this section not later than two years after the date of enactment of this Act.

SEC. 5. A bank or savings and loan association which violates a rule promulgated pursuant to this Act shall be subject to a civil penalty which shall not exceed $100 for each day of the violation.

* * *

[U.S.C., title 12, sec. 1881-1884.]

SCOPE

The rules contained in this Part—

(a) establish minimum standards for the installation, maintenance, and operation of security devices and procedures to discourage robberies, burglaries, and larcenies and to assist in the identification and apprehension of persons who commit such acts;

(b) establish time limits for compliance; and

(c) require the submission of reports.

DESIGNATION OF SECURITY OFFICER

On or before February 15, 1969 the board of directors of each financial institution shall designate an officer or other employee of the bank who shall be charged, subject to supervision by the board of directors, with responsibility for the installation, maintenance, and operation of security devices and for the development and administration of a security program which equal or exceed the standards prescribed by this Part.

SECTION 216.3—SECURITY DEVICES

(a) **Installation, maintenance, and operation of appropriate security devices.** Before January 1, 1970, the security officer of each financial institution, under such directions as shall be given him by the board of directors, shall survey the need for security devices in each of the institutions' offices and shall provide for the installation, maintenance, and operation, in each such office, of—

(1) a lighting system for illuminating, during the hours of darkness, the area around the vault, if the vault is visible from outside the banking office;

(2) tamper-resistant locks on exterior doors and exterior windows designed to be opened;

(3) an alarm system or other appropriate device for promptly notifying the nearest responsible law enforcement officers of an attempted or perpetrated robbery or burglary; and

(4) such other devices as the security officer, after seeking the advice of law enforcement officers, shall determine to be appropriate for discouraging robberies, burglaries, and larcenies and for assisting in the identification and apprehension of persons who commit such acts.

(b) **Considerations relevant to determining appropriateness.** For the purposes of subparagraph (4) of paragraph (a) of this section, considerations relevant to determining appropriateness include, but are not limited to—

(1) the incidence of crimes against the particular banking office and/or against financial institutions in the area in which the banking office is or will be located;

(2) the amount of currency or other valuables exposed to robbery, burglary, or larceny;

(3) the distance of the banking office from the nearest responsible law enforcement officers and the time required for such law enforcement officers ordinarily to arrive at the banking office;

(4) the cost of the security devices;

(5) other security measures in effect at the banking office; and

(6) the physical characteristics of the banking office structure and its surroundings.

(c) **Implementation.** It is appropriate for banking offices in areas with a high incidence of crime to install many devices which would not be practicable because of costs for small banking offices in areas substantially free of crimes against financial institutions. Each institution shall consider the appropriateness of installing, maintaining, and operating security devices which are expected to give a general level of bank protection at least equivalent to the standards described in Appendix A of this Part. In any case in which (on the basis of the factors listed in paragraph (b) or similar ones, the use of other measures, or the decision that technological change allows the use of other measures judged to give equivalent protection) it is decided not to install, maintain, and operate devices at least equivalent to these standards, the bank shall preserve in its records a statement of the reasons for such decision and forward a copy of that statement to the regulatory agency.

SECURITY PROCEDURES

(a) **Development and administration.** On or before July 15, 1969, each bank shall develop and provide for the administration of a security program to protect each of its banking offices from robberies, burglaries, and larcenies and to assist in the identification and apprehension of persons who commit such acts. This security program shall be reduced to writing, approved by the bank's board of directors, and retained by the bank in such form as will readily permit determination of its adequacy and effectiveness, and a copy shall be filed with the regulatory agency.

(b) **Contents of security programs.** Such security programs shall—

(1) provide for establishing a schedule for the inspection, testing, and servicing of all security devices installed in each banking office; provide for designating the officer or other employee who shall be responsible for seeing that such devices are inspected, tested, serviced, and kept in good working order; and require such officer or other employee to keep a record of such inspections, testings, and servicings;

(2) require that each banking office's currency be kept at a reasonable minimum and provide procedures for safely removing excess currency;

(3) require that the currency at each teller's station or window be kept at a reasonable minimum and provide procedures for safely removing excess currency and other valuables to a locked safe, vault, or other protected place;

(4) require that the currency at each teller's station or window include "bait" money, i.e., used Federal Reserve notes, the denominations, banks of issue, serial numbers, and series years of which are recorded, verified by a second officer or employee, and kept in a safe place;

(5) require that all currency, negotiable securities, and similar valuables be kept in a locked vault or safe during nonbusiness hours, that the vault or safe be opened at the latest time practicable before banking hours, and that the vault or safe be locked at the earliest time practicable after banking hours;

(6) provide, where practicable, for designation of a person or persons to open each banking office and require him or them to inspect the premises, to ascertain that no unauthorized persons are present, and to signal other employees that the premises are safe before permitting them to enter;

(7) provide for designation of a person or persons who will assure that all security devices are turned on and are operating during the periods in which such devices are intended to be used;

(8) provide for designation of a person or persons to inspect, after the closing hour, all areas of each banking office where currency, negotiable securities, or similar valuables are normally handled or stored in order to assure that such currency, securities, and valuables have been put away, that no unauthorized persons are

present in such areas, and that the vault or safe and all doors and windows are securely locked; and

(9) provide for training, and periodic retraining, of employees in their responsibilities under the security program, including the proper use of security devices and proper employee conduct during and after a robbery, in accordance with the procedures listed in Appendix B of this Part.

FILING OF REPORTS

(a) **Compliance reports.** As of the last business day in June of 1970, and as of the last business day in June of each calendar year thereafter, each institution shall file with the regulatory agency a statement certifying to its compliance with the requirements of this Part. The statement shall be dated and signed by the president, or cashier, or other managing officer of the bank and may be in a form substantially as follows:

> "I hereby certify, to the best of my knowledge and belief, that this bank has developed and administers a security program that equals or exceeds the standards prescribed by the Bank Protection Act; that such security program has been reduced to writing, approved by the bank's board of directors, and retained by the bank in such form as will readily permit determination of its adequacy and effectiveness; and that the bank security officer, after seeking the advice of law enforcement officers, has provided for the installation, maintenance, and operation of appropriate security devices, as prescribed by the Bank Protection Act in each of the bank's banking offices."

(b) **Reports on security devices.** On or before March 15, 1969, and upon such other occasions as the regulatory agency may specify, each bank shall file with the regulatory agency a report on Form P-1 (in duplicate) for each of its offices that is subject to this Part.

(c) **External crime reports.** Each time a robbery, burglary, or nonbank-employee larceny is perpetrated or attempted at a banking office, the bank shall, within a reasonable time, file a report in conformity with the requirements of Form P-2. One copy of such report shall be filed with the appropriate State supervisory authority and three copies of such report shall be filed with the Federal regulatory agency.

CORRECTIVE ACTION

Whenever the regulatory agency determines that the security devices or procedures used by a bank are deficient in meeting the requirements of this Part, or that the requirements of this Part should be varied in the circumstances of a particular banking office, it may take or require the bank to take necessary corrective action. If the regulatory agency determines that such corrective action is appropriate or necessary, the bank will be so notified and will be furnished a statement of what the bank must do to comply with the requirements of this Part.

PENALTY PROVISION

Pursuant to Section 5 of the Bank Protection Act of 1968, a bank that violates any provision of this Part shall be subject to a civil penalty not to exceed $100 for each day of the violation.

MINIMUM SECURITY DEVICES AND PROCEDURES (AMENDED)

Appendix A—Minimum Standards for Security Devices

Effective November 1, 1973, Appendix A *is amended* to read as follows:

In order to assure realization of maximum performance capabilities, all security devices utilized by a bank should be regularly inspected, tested, and serviced by competent persons. Actuating devices for surveillance systems and robbery alarms should be operable with the least risk of detection by unauthorized persons that can be practicably achieved.

(1) *Surveillance systems.* (i) *General.* Surveillance systems should be:

(A) equipped with one or more photographic, recording, monitoring, or like devices capable of reproducing images of persons in the banking office with sufficient clarity to facilitate (through photographs capable of being enlarged to produce a one-inch vertical head-size of persons whose images have been reproduced) the identification and apprehension of robbers or other suspicious persons;

(B) reasonably silent in operation; and

(C) so designed and constructed that necessary services, repairs or inspections can readily be made.

Any camera used in such a system should be capable of taking at least one picture every 2 seconds and, if it uses film, should contain enough unexposed film at all times to be capable of operating for not less than 3 minutes, and the film should be at least 16mm.

(ii) *Installation and operation of surveillance systems providing surveillance of other than walk-up or drive-in teller's stations or windows.* Surveillance devices for other than walk-up or drive-in teller's stations or windows should be:

(A) located so as to reproduce identifiable images of persons either leaving the banking office or in a position to transact business at each such station or window; and

(B) capable of actuation by initiating devices located at each teller's station or window.

(iii) *Installation and operation of surveillance systems providing surveillance of walk-up or drive-in teller's stations or windows.* Surveillance devices for walk-up or drive-in teller's stations or windows should be located in such a manner as to reproduce identifiable images of persons in a position to transact business at each such station or window and areas of such station or window that are vulnerable to robbery or larceny. Such devices should be capable of actuation by one or more initiating devices located within or in close proximity to such station or window. Such devices may be omitted in the case of a walk-up or drive-in teller's station or window in which the teller is effectively protected by a bullet-resistant barrier from persons outside the station or window. However, if the teller is vulnerable to larceny or robbery by members of the public who enter the banking office, the teller should have access to a device to actuate a surveillance system that covers the area of vulnerability or the exits to the banking office.

(2) *Robbery and burglary alarm systems.* (*i*) *Robbery alarm systems.* A robbery alarm system should be provided for each banking office at which the police ordinarily can arrive within 5

minutes after an alarm is actuated; all other banking offices should be provided with appropriate devices for promptly notifying the police that a robbery has occurred or is in progress. Robbery alarm systems should be:

(A) designed to transmit to the police, either directly or through an intermediary, a signal (not detectable by unauthorized persons) indicating that a crime against the banking office has occurred or is in progress;

(B) capable of actuation by initiating devices located at each teller's station or window (except walk-up or drive-in teller's stations or windows in which the teller is effectively protected by a bullet-resistant barrier and effectively isolated from persons, other than fellow employees, inside a banking office of which such station or window may be a part);

(C) safeguarded against accidental transmission of an alarm;

(D) equipped with a visual and audible signal capable of indicating improper functioning of or tampering with the system; and

(E) equipped with an independent source of power (such as a battery) sufficient to assure continuously reliable operation of the system for at least 24 hours in the event of failure of the usual source of power.

(ii) *Burglary alarm systems.* A burglary alarm system should be provided for each banking office. Burglary alarm systems should be:

(A) capable of detecting promptly an attack on the outer door, walls, floor, or ceiling of each vault, and each safe not stored in a vault, in which currency, negotiable securities, or similar valuables are stored when the office is closed, and any attempt to move any such safe;

(B) designed to transmit to the police, either directly or through an intermediary, a signal indicating that any such attempt is in progress; and for banking offices at which the police ordinarily cannot arrive within 5 minutes after an alarm is actuated, designed to actuate a loud sounding bell or other device that is audible inside the banking office and for a distance or approximately 500 feet outside the banking office;

(C) safeguarded against accidental transmission of an alarm;

(D) equipped with a visual and audible signal capable of

indicating improper functioning of or tampering with the system; and

(E) equipped with an independent source of power (such as a battery) sufficient to assure continuously reliable operation of the system for at least 80 hours in the event of failure of the usual source of power.

(3) *Walk-up and drive-in teller's stations or windows.* Walk-up and drive-in teller's stations or windows contracted for after February 15, 1969, should be constructed in such a manner that tellers are effectively protected by bullet-resistant barriers from robbery or larceny by persons outside such stations or windows. Such barriers should be of glass at least 1-3/16 inches in thickness,[1] or of material of at least equivalent bullet-resistance. Pass-through devices should be so designed and constructed as not to afford a person outside the station or window a direct line of fire at a person inside the station.

(4) *Vaults, safes, safe deposit boxes, night depositories, and automated paying or receiving machines.* Vaults, safes (if not to be stored in a vault), safe deposit boxes, night depositories, and automated paying or receiving machines, in any of which currency, negotiable securities, or similar valuables are to be stored when banking offices are closed, should meet or exceed the standards expressed in this section.

(i) *Vaults.* A vault is defined as a room or compartment that is designed for the storage and safekeeping of valuables and which has a size and shape which permits entrance and movement within by one or more persons. Other asset storage units which do not meet this definition of a vault will be considered as safes. Vaults contracted for after November 1, 1973,[2] should have walls, floor, and ceiling of reinforced concrete at least 12 inches in thickness.[3] The

[1]It should be emphasized that this thickness is merely bullet-resistant and not bulletproof.

[2]Vaults contracted for previous to this date should be constructed in conformance with all applicable specifications then in effect.

[3]The reinforced concrete should have: two grids of #5 (5/8" diameter) deformed steel bars located in horizontal and vertical rows in each direction to form grids not more than 4 inches on center; or two grids of expanded steel bank vault mesh placed parallel to the face of the walls, weighing at least 6 pounds per square foot to each grid, having a diamond pattern not more than 3" x 8"; or two grids of any other fabricated steel placed parallel to the face of the walls, weighing at least 6 pounds per square foot to each grid and having an open area not exceeding 4 inches on center. Grids are to be located not less than 6 inches apart and staggered in each direction. The concrete should develop an ultimate compression strength of at least 3,000 pounds per square inch.

vault door should be made of steel at least 3-1/2 inches in thickness, or other drill and torch resistant material, and be equipped with a dial combination lock, a time lock, and a substantial lockable day-gate. Electrical conduits into the vault should not exceed 1-1/2 inches in diameter and should be offset within the walls, floor, or ceiling at least once so as not to form a direct path of entry. A vault ventilator, if provided, should be designed with consideration of safety to life without significant reduction of the strength of the vault wall to burglary attack. Alternatively, vaults should be so designed and constructed as to afford at least equivalent burglary resistance.[4]

(ii) *Safes.* Safes contracted for after February 15, 1969, should weigh at least 750 pounds empty, or be securely anchored to the premises where located. The body should consist of steel, at least 1 inch in thickness, either cast or fabricated, with an ultimate tensile strength of 50,000 pounds per square inch and be fastened in a manner equal to a continuous 1/4 inch penetration weld having an ultimate tensile strength of 50,000 pounds per square inch. The door should be made of steel that is at least 1-1/2 inch in thickness, and at least equivalent in strength to that specified for the body; and the door should be equipped with a combination lock, or time lock, and with a relocking device that will effectively lock the door if the combination lock or time lock is punched. One hole not exceeding 1/2 inch diameter may be provided in the body to permit insertion of electrical conductors, but should be located so as not to permit a direct view of the door or locking mechanism. Alternatively, safes should be constructed of materials that will afford at least equivalent burglary resistance.

(iii) *Safe deposit boxes.* Safe deposit boxes used to safeguard customer valuables should be enclosed in a vault or safe meeting at least the above-specified minimum protection standards.

(iv) *Night depositories.* Night depositories (excluding envelope drops not used to receive substantial amounts of currency) contracted for after February 15, 1969, should consist of a receptacle

[4]Equivalent burglary-resistant materials for vaults do *not* include the use of a steel lining, either inside or outside a vault wall, in lieu of the specified reinforcement and thickness of concrete. Nonetheless, there may be instances, particularly where the construction of a vault of the specified reinforcement and thickness of concrete would require substantial structural modification of an existing building, where compliance with the specified standards would be unreasonable in cost. In those instances, the bank should comply with the procedure set forth in section 216.3(c) of Regulation P.

chest having cast or welded steel walls, top, and bottom, at least 1 inch in thickness; a steel door at least 1-1/2 inches in thickness, with a combination lock; and a chute, made of steel that is at least 1 inch in thickness, securely bolted or welded to the receptacle and to a depository entrance of strength similar to the chute. Alternatively, night depositories should be so designed and constructed as to afford at least equivalent burglary resistance.[5] Each depository entrance (other than an envelope drop slot) should be equipped with a lock. Night depositories should be equipped with a burglar alarm and be designed to protect against the "fishing" of a deposit from the deposit receptacle, and to protect against the "trapping" of a deposit for extraction.

(v) *Automated paying or receiving machines.* Except as hereinafter provided, cash dispensing machines (automated paying machines), including those machines which also accept deposits (automated receiving machines) contracted for after November 1, 1973, should weigh at least 750 pounds empty, or be securely anchored to the premises where located. Cash dispensing machines should contain, among other features, a storage chest having cast or welded steel walls, top, and bottom, at least one inch in thickness, with a tensile strength of at least 50,000 pounds per square inch. Any doors should be constructed of steel at least equivalent in strength to the storage chest and be equipped with a combination lock and with a relocking device that will effectively lock the door if the combination lock is punched. The housing covering the cash dispensing opening in the storage chest and the housing covering the mechanism for removing the cash from the storage chest, should be so designed as to provide burglary resistance at least equivalent to the storage chest and should also be designed to protect against the "fishing" of cash from the storage chest. The cash dispensing control and delivering mechanism (and, when applicable, cash deposit receipt mechanism) should be protected by steel, at least 1/2 inch in thickness, securely attached to the storage chest. A cash dispensing machine which also receives deposits should have a receptacle chest having the same burglary resistant characteristics as that of cash dispensing storage chest and should be designed to protect against the fishing and trapping of deposits. Necessary

[5]Equivalent burglary-resistant materials for night depositories include the use of one-fourth inch steel plate encased in 6 inches or more of concrete or masonry building wall.

ventilation for the automated machines should be designed so as to avoid significantly reducing the burglary resistance of the machines. The cash dispensing machine should also be designed so as to be protected against actuation by unauthorized persons, should be protected by a burglar alarm, and should be located in a well-lighted area. Alternatively, cash dispensing machines should be so designed and constructed as to afford at least equivalent burglary resistance.[6] A cash dispensing machine which is used inside a bank's premises only during bank business hours, and which is empty of currency and coin at all other times, should at least provide safeguards against "jimmying," unauthorized opening of the storage chest door, and against actuation by unauthorized persons.

---

[6]Equivalent burglary-resistant materials for cash dispensing machines include the use of 3/8 inch thick nickel stainless steel meeting American Society of Testing Materials (ASTM) Designation A 167-70, Type 304, in place of 1 inch thick steel, if other criteria are satisfied.

PROTECTION PLANNING

PERSONNEL HIRING

Any organization is only as efficient as the personnel who compose its work force. In the case of a financial institution, this statement can be taken one step further. The organization's ability to control monetary loss is only as great as the intelligence and honesty of its employees.

Banks, by their very nature, must insure that only applicants with excellent moral turpitude, as well as intelligence and common sense are placed on the payroll.

The point at which these factors must be maintained is at the time of application of the prospective employee, and before this applicant is actually hired.

The first step is to have a comprehensive and detailed employment application which requires the applicant to indicate a brief, yet concise, history of his adult life, with particular attention to prior employment.

The applicant, as well as giving routine personal data, must indicate all places of prior employment, including name of employer, dates of employment, type of job, name of immediate supervisor, salary, and reason for leaving.

This information should be as completely verified as possible by the bank's personnel department, prior to the actual employment of the applicant, even though in a "probationary" status.

Particular attention should be paid to gaps in employment dates, failure to name immediate supervisors, situations where the job being applied for draws a much smaller salary than the applicant's present job, and where the reason for leaving is ambiguous, such as "didn't get along," "didn't like boss or fellow workers," or failure to conform to company rules."

Because of bonding company requirements, as well as Federal

statute regulations, each applicant should be asked if he has ever been convicted of a crime. Irregardless of the answer, the bank should insure that a criminal record check is conducted. This may be done in one of two ways.

1. Fingerprint the applicant and send the prints to the F.B.I. Identification Division in Washington. The F.B.I. is again authorized to check prints submitted by federally chartered or insured financial institutions. This is the best way to insure a thorough check of the applicant, because the F.B.I. files will indicate an arrest by any law enforcement agency in the United States. Since S.E.C. regulations now require financial institutions to fingerprint all employees handling securities, ownership of a fingerprinting kit may save time and allow for the convenient filing of all employees fingerprints.

2. Submit the applicant's name to your local police department for a record examination. This will generally require a signed authorization from the applicant allowing the police department to reveal any criminal record he may have. This authorization can be obtained as a matter of routine when the applicant first applies. Any applicant who refuses to sign this authorization should of course not be considered further for employment.

This second method is only partially effective, because the local police department will only have a record of the applicant if he was arrested and charged by the local department. Therefore, it is only of value in checking applicants who have lived and worked in the local community throughout their adult lives. It is valueless for an applicant who is moving to your community, even from the next county, let alone from another state. Currently proposed "privacy" legislation may eliminate the use of this second method in the near future, by prohibiting dissemination of criminal conviction information to prospective employers, even with a signed authorization from the applicant.

All applicants should of course be given a routine credit bureau screening. Many times credit investigations will reveal the possibility of the applicant's involvement in a criminal act, but their principal function is to assist in verifying the applicant's prior employment, his credit worthiness, and his present indebtedness. It will give a good indication of his ability to live within his means, and an idea of how valuable he considers his credit reputation.

Most employment applications will probably have a place for the applicant to list personal references. You may wish to contact these references, but take their recommendations with a grain of salt. After all, who would put down the name of someone who knew of their character defects as a reference for employment.

Be sure to verify all prior employment claimed by the applicant for a period of at least five years. This includes dates of employment. Insure that there are no unexplained gaps. You will undoubtedly encounter some difficulty here. More frequently employers are refusing to divulge any information about former employees, for fear of civil liabilities, or of possible violation of the "Fair Credit Reporting Act." Many employers will actually cover up illegal acts committed by the applicant while in their employment. This is a good reason for never limiting an applicant investigation to just checking with former employers.

The ultimate answer to this entire problem is the use of a pre-employment polygraph or psychological stress evaluator (P.S.E.) examination of the applicant. This tool is being used more and more by financial institutions to test applicants for positions of financial trust.

The polygraph or P.S.E. examination for this purpose is against the law in some states. It is wise to check your particular state laws before considering this method.

A pre-employment polygraph or P.S.E. test can discover not only prior dishonesty, but a latent tendency to dishonesty. The test, however, is only as good as the examiner who conducts it. You will need a conscientious, well-trained and objective examiner to read the chart and correctly interpret the findings.

One final area to be considered is the medical aspect. The applicant should either be required to provide a report of a recent physical examination or the bank should arrange for this service to be performed at bank expense prior to hiring.

The latter method is preferable, as the applicant's doctor may have a reluctance to reveal medical problems adversely affecting employment, due to the doctor-patient relationship. This may be particularly true in the case of drug users.

The employment application itself should of course contain a question regarding drug use by the applicant. In addition, a successful method of screening out drug users is to inform all applicants that prospective employees will be given a medical examination, including urinalysis.

Coupling this statement with one advising that all applicants will be fingerprinted and have a polygraph or P.S.E. examination will greatly assist your personnel department in screening out undesirables.

PERSONNEL RECHECKING

After employment, the employee is seldom examined during the remainder of his employment. This, in many instances, is a mistake. Employees of financial institutions have the same needs and desires as those of every other human being. They can become as financially over-extended and caught up in money problems as the rest of us. Most employees, when faced with adversity, will resist the temptation; some cannot and some will not.

One of the earliest tools available to the employer is the "Credit Inquiry Inventory. This means that you no longer treat as routine, credit inquiries from outside lending agencies concerning an employee of the bank. Keep records of these inquiries. A rapid rise in the number and frequency of such requests indicates an employee is in financial trouble. When this happens, there is a need to find out why. Most banks allow employees to borrow money at a discounted rate of interest. If your employee is not availing himself of this opportunity, or has used up his loan availability with the bank, and is out looking for other sources of credit, you may have a serious problem, leading to bankruptcy or dishonesty by the employee.

Another tool readily available to those banks providing free employee checking accounts to their personnel is a spot check of account statements on a random basis, by the bank auditor. Questions regarding unexplained deposits can easily be resolved by checking original deposit tickets and associated items. Large checks can be reviewed in the same manner.

Of course, the best answer to this problem is the alert, conscientious and competent supervisor who knows his employees, and to whom they freely can bring their problems, knowing that he will listen and provide good counsel.

DRUG ABUSE

The average drug addict needs about $10,000 a year to support his habit. To get it, he must steal merchandise worth approximately

$50,000. He does not care from whom he steals. If he works for you, or with you, he will steal from your company. It is important, therefore, that you learn to recognize the drug addict.

A drug addict is a human being in need of medical care. Without such care, the addict loses his self-respect and the respect of his family and friends. He threatens the well-being of his company and his co-workers.

If you can identify the addict, you have taken the first step toward his rehabilitation and toward the safety and security of your bank. The addict needs help.

The following indications do not necessarily reflect drug addiction. They may reflect other diseases. Nevertheless, symptoms or indications deserve attention and continued observation.

The most easily identifiable addict wears sunglasses to hide dilated pupils, wears long-sleeved shirts to hide needle marks, often has a running nose, perspires profusely, scratches himself constantly, nods his head frequently, urinates often, and is a chain smoker.

Addicts use a variety of drugs; OPIATES such as opium, morphine, heroin, and codeine; STIMULANTS such as amphetamines and cocaine; DEPRESSANTS such as barbiturates and other tranquilizers; HALLUCINOGENS such as marijuana, L.S.D., morning glory seeds, S.T.P. and mescaline.

Major symptoms or indicators of drug abuse are the following:

A. General Indicators
   1. Poor attendance
   2. Unkempt appearance
   3. Habitual borrowing of money
   4. Deterioration of work performance
   5. Use of narcotics jargon

B. External Physical Indicators
   1. Dilated pupils (often hidden by sunglasses)
   2. Bloodstains on shirt sleeves
   3. Needle marks (usually hidden by long-sleeved shirt)
   4. Soreness or ulcers under nose (from sniffing)
   5. Running nose
   6. Profuse perspiration
   7. Tremors or chills
   8. Goose flesh on body
   9. Chronic dry cough

10. Rapid loss of weight
11. Vomiting

C. Behavioral Indicators
1. Slurred speech
2. Stupor or drowsiness
3. Constant scratching
4. Frequent nodding of head
5. Irritability, restlessness, unusual outbreaks of temper
6. Suffers from constipation
7. Urinates frequently
8. Extreme fatigue
9. Chain smoking, craving for sweets and extreme thirst
10. Drunken appearance (without odor of alcohol)

THE BANK GUARD FORCE

All financial institutions will at some point contemplate the hiring of a guard or guard force. This may be because of a high incidence of robbery, or of internal pilferage, or for one of many reasons too numerous to mention.

When considering this question, the bank must decide what service the guard is to perform. Is he to be used to protect the premises from after-hour intrusion, to keep order during the business day, to prevent hold-up and other fraudulent attack, or to act as a dispenser of information?

Most guards can be expected to handle several minor functions, with one exception. If he is hired to prevent robbery, this is the only function he can and should be expected to handle. He cannot provide a deterrent to the bandit, while helping an elderly customer to find the rest room, or playing with children while their mother conducts her banking business.

The next consideration is whether to place the guard in uniform and arm him with a revolver. The answer to this depends on your decision as to his principal use. If he works after hours for premises protection, he should be in uniform and armed. If he is to be used to keep order in the lobby during open hours, and to act as a source of information for customers, he should be uniformed and not armed. For his own protection however, insure that his uniform in no way resembles a "police" uniform. In case of an armed robbery, the robber will probably shoot him first if he looks like a "policeman" who would offer a threat to the robber, and your guard would have no way to defend himself.

If you intend to use the guard as a defense against armed attacks, it is best that you either consider hiring an off-duty regular police officer in uniform, or a guard in plainclothes who is armed and trained to handle the weapon.

Remember, if you hire a private bank guard and arm him, you must train him in the use of that weapon. If he ever uses the weapon and accidently inflicts harm on an innocent party, you will be involved in a significant civil liability suit. Your only defense is production of written training records showing firearms training (up to date) by date and length of instruction provided to that guard.

In assembling a guard force, you will get just what you are willing to pay for, and this is the point where most banks forget the economic facts of life. Based on the pay scales of 1975, if you offer an annual salary of $6,500 to $8,000, you will get applicants who are retired, generally from the local police department or a private guard service. They may possibly have some physical impairment which led to early retirement but they can still function capably for use as lobby fixtures and information passers. If you want a guard to protect your premises, you must raise your sights.

The $9,000 to 11,000 range will provide you with a younger more intelligent man. This pay range with proper selection will provide the uniformed, armed, capable man for night premises protection.

To obtain the competent individual necessary for armed robbery deterrent, you will have to pay at least the going rate for starting police officers in your community, normally $12,000 to 14,000. Remember that you have to train this man and keep him trained.

Any of these employees will of course cost more than an annual salary. They are eligible for all the fringe benefits given to other employees of your bank. They take vacations, and have weekends and holidays off, and must be replaced. This means additional personnel with their incumbent costs.

If your bank cannot accept these costs, and you still need and want a guard force, you must consider a contract with a private service. There are many fine private guard companies in this country. They have years of experience and have provided conscientious service with few complaints. There are also many unsatisfactory guard services, who hire men cheaply, overwork them, and go out of business rapidly.

A good contract service will provide the guard, arm him if you so desire (and provide his training with the weapon), put him in uniform or not, again as you desire. You need not worry about holidays, weekends and vacations. They will insure his replacement during these periods. In fact, if he is late arriving for work, they will put in a substitute to cover until his arrival.

We must also point out the disadvantages. From the economic standpoint, the private guard service must recruit its personnel from the same sources you would if you established a bank guard force. Under the minimum wage law, they must pay $2.30 per hour, or $4,500 per year. This means they get the same type applicants you would have—the retired and the slightly disabled. They must pay more to recruit the better qualified physically and mentally.

The private service is a profit making operation with the resultant overhead costs of any large organization. If the guard gets $2.30 per hour, your cost will be at least $3.50 per hour ($7,000 per year). So you get a $4,500 guard, and pay $2,500 for the freedom from worry. The more physically and mentally qualified guard you desire, the more your cost will rise proportionately.

The next area to consider is continuity. This results in what is usually called, "The Tarzan Principle." A poor contract service in bidding for your business will try to present the lowest bid consistent with acceptable service. The salesman will probably tell you that for this price his company will furnish you a guard "that looks like Tarzan, and can investigate like J. Edgar Hoover." This is about what you will get for the first two weeks after you have signed an agreement. At the beginning of the third week, however, he will disappear, and you will find in his place a guard "that looks like J. Edgar Hoover and can investigate like Tarzan." This is the type of guard that will remain in your office until you are willing to pay for better, and let the contract company know it.

The reputable companies will try their utmost to leave the same guard in your bank, and are often able to do this. However, this is not a thing you can control. They have employees who retire, are promoted, resign and are fired just like everyone else, and when something of this nature happens, it causes a large wave of transfers of personnel between clients. Consequently, just when you get to know the man and how he operates in your office your are suddenly faced with a stranger and have to start teaching the "house rules" all over again.

SECURITY OF THE COMPUTER CENTER

The protection of the computer center should be considered as the most important function of the security officer in a financial institution. The physical protection of the center should far exceed that given to vaults and safes, where currency is stored and handled. Yet, we find that the Bank Protection Act does not mention anything about protection of this asset. We have become so involved in protecting the money, which can easily be replaced, that we forget that the very life of our organization, our customers' records and the internal records of the bank are stored in the computer, and can, if lost or destroyed, literally force us out of business.

Think for a moment, how would your bank function if unable to retrieve and use the stored information for a day, a week, or even a month. Would your customers be willing to cease all financial transactions for these periods to allow you to replace equipment, restore vital financial records, and resume business, or would they go to your competitor?

In the coming days of Electronic Funds Transfer, Point of Sale Terminals, and On Line financial transactions, the computer is the one and only tool upon which these programs can function. Therefore, the security of the computer center, including all information and equipment should now become a prime concern of every financial institution security officer.

For most of you, your computer site is already constructed and any changes in its physical layout will be almost impossible.

We still are faced with remnants of the days when it was traditional to enclose the center in glass, so visiting dignitaries and customers could watch the lights flash and the tapes and discs spin. If your center is one of these type installations, you will have a problem to which the only solution is a complete reconstruction project, and selling that to your management may present an awesome task.

If you have not yet installed your computer, or if you are upgrading your systems and equipment, consider these factors in your planning.

Begin with a survey of the planned site starting with the location and the perimeter of the area involved.

The site should be located in an interior area of the building so that no side includes one of the existing walls particularly one containing windows. If this is not possible, install exterior mesh or grill work over these windows to preclude unauthorized access or the hurling of destructive missiles through the glass.

The site, if located in an existing building over one story in height, should be located on the top floor. High rise office buildings are constructed to resemble a swiss cheese with holes for conduit and servicing of heating and cooling systems, and false ceilings. A computer is as prone to destruction by water as by fire. A broken water pipe on an upper floor will result in water cascading through the ceilings of lower floors and you will find your computer site inundated in short order. If you must build on a lower floor, provide for plastic sheeting to cover the equipment and plenty of outside drainage from under the false floor of the site.

The site should be equipped with an automatic fire sensing and protection system which will react to the slightest indication of excessive heat or smoke. Of course this requires a no smoking rule in the center and requires strict enforcement of this rule.

The site should be unmarked so that its function is not advertised to the public. Why should we invite unauthorized intrusion.

A tight access control system is another fundamental security principle. Points of access should be limited to one or two controlled doors depending on the size of the site and the number of employees. This should not, however, preclude emergency exit doors which can be strategically placed to permit egress of authorized personnel in the event of fire or other emergency evacuaton. These doors must have appropriate security hardware to prevent intrusion and should have alarm systems to detect unauthorized entry.

The regular access doors can be controlled by several methods including double door entry systems observed by guards or closed circuit T.V. The locking mechanisms include combination or card control panels or a combination of both.

A continuous videotape system can be used to record all entry and exit through the access doors.

No visitors should be allowed inside the site. To permit such access not only invites possible trouble, but may leave management open to a negligence suit for non-protection of proprietary information.

The tapes and discs on which all proprietary information is stored should be kept in a library within the computer center, under the control of a full-time librarian. This library should be in the form of a regular concrete vault with fire door and combination locks. This vault should be completely fireproof.

The librarian checks in and out all tapes and disc packs and maintains a complete record of their use by name, date and time. No person should be permitted in this library except the librarian.

Where practical, tapes, discs and printouts containing highly sensitive proprietary information should be segregated within the library and special protective measures for their storage and release should be established.

Plans should be developed to specify actions to be taken by site personnel in the event of emergencies such as bomb threats, unauthorized intrusions, fire, water or natural disasters.

Another very important aspect of security planning is storage of duplicable (grandfather) tapes and discs. These should be located away from the office site, in another safe location, such as a vault in a separate building, to insure that if the computer facility is destroyed, the lost information can be reconstructed.

Arrangements should be made with another computer site for possible use of their equipment on a time-sharing basis if your equipment is rendered inoperable at any time. Be sure however, that their equipment is completely compatible with yours. If their tape drive units won't handle your tapes, you have gained nothing in such an arrangement.

Each security system will have to be tailored to your particular installation and should be the result of a comprehensive security survey. In doing this survey, remember that security planning is for the best protection consistent with cost and usage. The computer site needs people to make it work. If your security program results in denial of needed movement to authorized personnel into and within the site, you will effectively hamstring the entire computer operation. You must effectively balance this against the requirement for protection.

Let us consider for a moment the people who will work in the site and where they fit in this picture.

These employees are a special breed of technicians. They are not bookkeepers and we should not treat them as such. They will probably not conform to our idea of "bankers", nor should they. There will be a tendency on the part of management to grumble because they work strange hours, do not wear ties, and do not comport themselves in an "accepted fashion." A programmer involved in a complex problem may work 48 hours straight to come up with a solution. He will then go home to bed for 2 days. If we refuse to accept this fact and attempt to discipline him because he does not "punch the time clock" like the rest of the employees, we will insure a continual turnover of site personnel and a disgruntled working staff. A disgruntled computer employee will cause more problems than bombers, terrorists or any other possible external threat to the computer system.

If, for any *valid* reason it is necessary to terminate a disgruntled or non-performing site employee, this should be done without prior warning. As soon as he is dismissed, he should not be allowed to return to the computer site for any reason. Any personal effects should be inventoried and crated by a supervisor and sent or delivered to his home.

A final consideration in computer site protection is good housekeeping. The site must be kept clean at all times. Waste paper, outdated printouts, and old punch cards should be removed at least twice a day. They should be destroyed by shredding or compacting, preferably both, to prevent confidential information from falling into the wrong hands.

ALARM SYSTEMS

Under the Bank Protection Act of 1968, all federally insured or chartered financial institutions are required to consider the installation of an alarm system or other appropriate device for notifying law enforcement officials that a robbery is in progress or has been committed.

This determination is to be based on several factors including:

1. Incidence of crimes against the specific office.
2. Amount of currency exposed to robbery, burglary or larceny.
3. Distance of the office from the nearest available law enforcement agency.
4. Cost of the system.
5. Other security measures in effect at the office.
6. Physical characteristics of the office.

In making a decision, each financial institution was required to contact the appropriate law enforcement agency serving their area, for recommendations.

The term "other appropriate device" has never been adequately defined, and was apparently meant to cover those situations in which an alarm sending system was not feasible.

For example, many banks located in rural areas are served by a county sheriff, whose office may be located 20 miles from the bank. The feasibility of running alarm lines to the sheriff's office is negligible in view of cost, and distance. The banker, however, may wish to install some type of alarm signal connected to a local commercial business establishment adjacent to his bank. Should his bank be robbed, the signal would notify his neighbor to call the sheriff. Such a situation could be considered to fall under the "other appropriate device" criteria.

For financial institutions in urban areas, with full-time police protection, the decision to install alarm devices becomes more meaningful. If the decision is made to install such devices, additional consideration must be given to whether the alarm system should be connected directly to the police department or through a central station monitoring company.

In many cases, the local police department will not allow termination of the alarm system at their facility, and the central station will be the only available means of service. If your community allows termination of the lines at the police department, the following advantages and disadvantages should be considered.

TERMINATION AT POLICE DEPARTMENT

Possible Advantages

1. Many communities will allow financial institutions to place an alarm termination board in the police dispatcher's area. The banks must bear the cost of this board and its installation, but the police personnel will monitor the board as part of their assigned duties *at no further cost to the bank(s)* for this service.

2. The police dispatcher, upon viewing the alarm signal, is in a position to immediately dispatch police units to respond to the bank, thus saving valuable seconds which may make the difference in apprehension of the robber.

Possible Disadvantages

1. The police dispatcher is required to perform many other

duties besides monitoring the alarm board. In the event that he is otherwise engaged in these duties, he may miss seeing the alarm signal, when first transmitted.

2. Most termination boards are equipped with a *red* signal indicating an actual alarm, and a yellow signal indicating some type of electronic trouble on the line. The average dispatcher will not take the time to distinguish between these two signals and will send police units to the bank in either case. In the event of line trouble, you will find your lobby filled with police time and again until the trouble is identified and repaired. This causes consternation among your customers and employees, and angers the officers responding to the bank time after time.

3. The bank, of course, is paying monthly fees for the signal grade phone wire running between your bank and the police department. The bank will also be paying for a service contract with the equipment company who installed the system, to service and test the lines. Most equipment companies will claim to have 24-hour service availability in the event of line trouble. Don't be surprised when this fails to materialize; and you will find your system is compromised for the entire period it is waiting for repair. In addition, the equipment company ties into lines supplied by the telephone company. When line trouble develops, you will find yourself in the middle of a jurisdictional dispute. The equipment company will blame the phone company and vice-versa. In the meantime, the police department will be requesting immediate repair, and you will be without alarm service, during this entire period.

4. At some point in time, after your alarm has been installed, one of your local politicians will become aware that the community is providing you with a free service, namely the monitoring of your system by the police department. Since politicians are always in search of additional revenue, you will suddenly find that this free service has been cancelled. The city will begin billing you for the monitoring service, and may also institute a kicker called "false alarm charges." This means that everytime police are dispatched to your bank, and no *robbery* or *burglary* has occurred, you will be required to pay a fee for having transmitted a false alarm. Now, if you will recall paragraph 2, herein, and the dispatcher who sends police responding to the yellow trouble signal, it becomes apparent that your fees for that originally free service, have made a police alarm system a very expensive proposition.

TERMINATION AT A CENTRAL STATION COMPANY

Possible Advantages

1. One company installs the equipment, pays for the phone lines, and monitors the alarm board. For this service you pay a fixed monthly or yearly rate.

2. Since the company's business is alarm service, you can normally expect 24-hour maintenance and repair of your system. This includes resolution of differences between the central station and the telephone company as to responsibility for line trouble. The central station rents a large number of phone lines, and is therefore a preferred service customer of the phone company. Problems between the two are rapidly resolved.

3. Personnel monitoring your alarm are hired to do nothing but this job. Their alarm circuits also differentiate between an actual alarm and line trouble. They can tell the difference and will not send police in the event of the latter problem.

Possible Disadvantages

1. Upon receipt of a valid alarm signal, the central station must call the police, at the *correct* police department covering your bank. The time taken to make the call and pass the information is time gained by the bandit to complete his depredations and escape apprehension.

2. Generally, fees for service from a central station company will far exceed the cost of a police system (equipment supplier service contract, telephone company line costs) if the police monitoring service is free, and there are no false alarm charges.

ALARM SENDING DEVICES—ROBBERY

Buttons—These are the cheapest items to install at teller stations. They result in a medium frequency of false alarms due to accidental tripping. They are generally also the least used by the teller in the event of an actual hold-up, because the robber is more likely to see the movement of the teller's hand, and tellers will usually not take the chance.

Footrails—These are in the middle cost range to install. They cause a large number of false alarms due to accidental tripping by the teller's foot movements during the course of the banking day. The teller will usually have no fear of activating this type of alarm in the presence of the robber.

Bill Traps—These are the most expensive type of sending units. Small chance of accidental tripping and therefore very few false alarms. The teller has no hesitation in activating this device during the course of the robbery. If the bandit is rifling the teller drawers, he will trip the alarm by his own actions. The basic drawback is the requirement that the electrical connection between the leads from the teller truck to the counter, must be correctly joined each day to insure proper operation of the system.

ALARM SENDING DEVICES—BURGLARY

Vault Door Contact Switch—Sends alarm if vault door is opened while system is set in alarm condition. Has no value against attack through any area of the vault but the door.

Sound Sensor—This type system transmits an alarm when sound is heard inside the vault while in an alarm condition. The sensor is normally tuned to eliminate regular outside noises which would carry through to the sensor. If your bank is in a heavy industrial area, your sensor has probably been so lowly tuned to prevent accidental tripping that a quiet burglar can successfully attack your vault without causing an alarm drop.

Heat Sensor—This sensor transmits an alarm when the temperature in the vault builds beyond a selected range. This sensor was developed in answer to the thermal lance (burning bar). It has no effect against other methods of vault attack.

Intrusion Alarm—This sensor may be used inside the vault or in the lobby area. It operates on a motion principle and transmits the signal on ascertaining movement. Many of them can be set off accidentally by the movement of small rodents, draperies by draft, etc.

ALARM LINE COMPROMISE

Most alarm systems today use signal grade telephone lines to transmit the alarm signal between the bank and the police (or central station) department. When the alarm system is "set", a direct current provided by commercial electrical service (or emergency battery power) is continuously fed through this line.

When any of the alarm sensors described above (or the hold-up devices in the case of a robbery alarm) are activated, they cause an interruption of this flow of current, which activates the light or needle on the monitor board.

If the bandit or burglar can obtain access to the telephone line used for signal transmission, he can introduce his own battery power onto the line and attack your premises without fear of discovery. To make this job more difficult for him, you should insure that the signal phone lines enter your premises underground, and are carried in conduit within your premises. These lines will terminate at the telephone junction box along with your regular phone service line. Therefore, this junction box should be located in a locked area within the bank. In addition, the alarm lines terminating in the box should *not* be visibly tagged as to their purpose.

Other more secure type line systems are available to you from your alarm equipment supplier at additional cost. Some systems will use a variable current, or a tone signal or a combination of both to stop the battery using burglar.

You may wish to consider the additional expense of these systems, depending on the location and burglary incidents in the neighborhood of your bank.

SURVEILLANCE SYSTEMS

One of the greatest aids to the police in the apprehension of bank robbers is a good photograph of the robber taken during the commission of the robbery by a bank surveillance camera.

Camera systems are as numerous and varied as any other of today's products. They range in size and shape from 8MM movie cameras to 70MM sequential still cameras. The 8MM cameras are presently not allowed by law to be used for bank surveillance purposes, but they can be used for internal control purposes in non-lobby areas such as the cash and securities storage vaults.

In addition to cameras, numerous suppliers are now promoting closed circuit television monitors and tape devices.

If you have decided on a surveillance system, you may wish to consider these factors.

SIZE OF CAMERA

8MM Movie—presently not authorized because the quality of the photograph is not generally sufficient for positive identification and reproduction. This item may come under consideration for authorization because it is inexpensive to purchase and install, film and servicing costs are low, and the general feeling is that a picture from this type camera is better than no pictures at all.

16MM Movie—this camera is probably the most widely used throughout the banking industry. It provides generally recognizable and reproducible photographs. The system is moderately priced, film cost is not a major expense factor, and film processing is locally available.

35MM Still—coming into wider use for the clarity and reproducibility of the photographs. This camera takes still photos in rapid sequence during the robbery. One camera can usually cover an area requiring two movie cameras in a bank lobby. Film cost and processing costs are greater. Also, after the robbery, the place where the film can be processed is generally not locally available.

70MM Still—expensive to purchase, expensive to operate, very few locally available processors to handle the film after a robbery. This camera gives extremely fine, clear photographs of the robber(s), and one camera will normally cover an entire bank lobby.

METHODS OF ACTIVATION

Hold-up Alarm

Most surveillance cameras are tied into the hold-up alarm system. When a teller activates the alarm, the camera commences operation and continues until it either runs out of film or the alarm is reset.

Advantages

This type of system hook-up affords low film cost and a generally low maintenance cost factor.

Disadvantages

If the teller fails to (or refuses to) activate the hold-up alarm until after the bandit has left the bank, the camera is valueless and you have wasted money to install it in the first place. The refusal to activate the alarm will normally be justified by the teller's statement that "the camera makes so much noise, I felt the robber would hear it and know I had set off the alarm." Everytime you have a false alarm, the film will run down or run out. If you forget to change film, the camera will be empty when a real robbery occurs.

Remember also that all film ages and becomes useless. Film must be replaced at least every six months in the camera, and the old, unused film destroyed. The principal drawback from the alarm activated camera is that it is only useful during a robbery situation. If you are going to spend money for a camera system, why not get one which you can use all the time.

Continuous Sequential Action with Hold-up Alarm Triggered Override

This system permits the taking of photographs in sequence at a selected time interval throughout the banking day. Most systems of this nature are set to take a photograph every 30 seconds or one minute. There is a hold-up alarm override which, when the hold-up alarm is activated, changes the camera to rapid sequence (or movie) and takes continuous photographs of the robbery until the film is exhausted or the alarm is reset

Advantages

Even though the teller fails (or refuses to) activate the hold-up alarm, you should get at least one or two photos of the bandit, taken on the normal sequence timing. Since the camera film will be changed and processed on a regular basis (normally once a week), you will not have a problem of overage film or an empty camera in the event of a robbery. By processing and reviewing each week's film, your equipment servicer can determine any camera repairs or realignments necessary, on an immediate basis.

The photographs can be used for many additional purposes, such as:

a) fraudulent check passers
b) larcenies
c) flim-flam and short change artists
d) pigeon drop subjects
e) fraudulent depositor claims
f) internal employee operations reviews

By retention and storage of processed film, you have ready recall of incidents which may arise in dispute later, such as the depositor who denies making a savings withdrawal 15 months ago, or the fraudulent government check which takes at least six months to come back dishonored from the Treasury Dept. If you use a 16MM camera system and your bank normally uses 16MM microfilming equipment for internal record work, the surveillance film can be viewed and pictures made on your regular microfilm viewing equipment without additional cost for purchase of photo editing/viewing equipment, and without the cost of regular glossy photographic prints being made by the film processor.

Disadvantages

The principal disadvantage is film cost for purchase and processing. For a 16MM system, each camera will require a film outlay of about $500 a year. Storage room for processed film (and the internal cost in tied up space) may also be considered a disadvantage.

CLOSED CIRCUIT TELEVISION

The facts concerning the cameras as far as method of activation will generally apply to television systems. The variances in the two systems are size and film/tape use.

The size of the television camera and its coverage is directly related to lens size. The larger the lens the greater the coverage.

The area of film versus video tape is the principal area of controversy. Film once used can never be used again. Video tape can be reused, but only for a limited number of times before it becomes blurry and distorted. Never believe a salesman who says you can reuse video tape forever. Normally a tape will last for about 30 reuses before beginning to distort.

For a continuous surveillance system, you must have a large quantity of expensive tapes to support it. Two or three tapes being reused in succession will mean you can only retain the work of a few days in storage for back reference. This will not help you to catch the checkpasser who defrauded you two weeks ago.

THE SURVEILLANCE EQUIPMENT SUPPLIER

The optimum surveillance equipment supplier for your purposes is a company which handles all facets of the program.

He installs and maintains the cameras, provides the film, processes the film, reviews the film to ascertain necessary camera repairs or adjustments, makes any prints from the film you may desire, and stores the processed film for you, if you do not have the space to do this yourself.

In this way, he is responsible for the total surveillance system and finished product.

If you do not have such a system offered, you must expect the following problems.

Your bank is robbed and the teller activates the alarm and surveillance system. The robber finishes his task and flees. The police arrive and immediately want the film from the camera. Your personnel remove the film and hand it to the policeman who then asks, "Where do I take it?" Being unsure yourself, you call the camera supplier. He tells you to send it to New York because he does not have a local processor. The policeman wants pictures *now* and doesn't want it mailed to New York, because he must maintain a "chain of custody" on the evidence. At this point, you start phoning local camera shops to find the nearest processor. With 16MM film, this is no great problem, but if you have 35MM or 70MM you have a real problem, unless you are located in a large urban area. If you are lucky, you find a processor and the policeman leaves with your film. He returns in two hours to show you a handful of black illegible prints and disgustedly asks what happened.

A call to your camera supplier informs you that the camera was functioning, it must have been bad film.

A call to your film supplier confirms that the film was OK, it must have been a bad camera, or the film was incorrectly processed.

A call to the processor advises you that it's not his fault, and inasmuch as he processed it on a rush order as a favor to you and the police, you really have no cause for complaint anyway.

There are now two choices. You can either replace your whole costly surveillance system and chalk it up to experience, or you can hope the robber comes back again to give you a second chance to photograph him and prove that the system will really work!

PROTECTION OF ASSETS

CHECKS—MISUSE & ABUSE

NEW AND/OR FRAUDULENT ACCOUNTS

The place to stop our biggest loss problem (unsatisfactory accounts) is in the beginning, at the new accounts desk.

Not too long ago, if a person wanted to open a checking account, he was required to furnish references, including a bank reference. Letters of inquiry were written. After the references replied with acceptable recommendations, the account was opened. However, the large volume of new accounts handled daily by some banks makes it somewhat impractical to investigate thoroughly each applicant for a personal account.

There are two types of persons opening accounts today that are a threat to ourselves and merchants. Number one: the habitual overdraft customer who moves from bank to bank as his return check problems become a potential loss factor to communities and banks, thus the bank is forced to close his account. Number two: possibly the most dangerous to the bank is the person opening the fraudulent account.

The best weapon in coping with fraudulent check problems is, of course, preventing the crime from occurring.

This calls for constant alertness on the part of the institute handling checks. A few minutes spent in verifying identification is a precautionary measure which means the safe-guarding of huge amounts of money.

Teamwork is considered essential in all fields of endeavor, from a sand lot baseball game to a flight to the moon. Without it we would fail. If the banks were as organized as our criminal element, soon the check fraud could be cut to a minimum. If you don't open a fraudulent account it is virtually impossible to defraud your bank.

The same care and investigation should go into opening a new checking account as goes into a new loan application, since the loss potential for the community is much higher on a bad checking account than on a loan.

The common objective of the new account swindler is to obtain a supply of checks and deposit tickets. Usually a small cash deposit will put the thief in business. After he receives his checks and deposit tickets, he then has two ways to work.

Number one, he may pass the worthless checks on local merchants and/or the bank. Number two, he may use the deposit tickets to deposit worthless checks and less cash or split the deposits.

He may also deposit large worthless checks and then withdraw the funds, if for some reason the funds are not being held by the bank until the deposited checks are cleared or collected.

He may go one step further and open a savings account and use the savings pass book as an added identification. In any event he has a thriving business for usually less than $100.00.

As banks become more sophisticated with their procedures, so do the ballpoint bandits. Corporate or business accounts lure the more wily thief. It Is a known fact that it is much easier to pass a business payroll check than a personal check.

In many cases, to make the new account look legitimate, the person will rent a store room or an office and have a phone installed, and letterheads printed. This type of fraud can possibly take several months to set up before a big hit. In these cases the take usually exceeds $10,000.00.

Some swindlers open accounts solely to facilitate the negotiation of stolen and forged items, such as U.S. Treasury checks, bonds, etc.

To avert such losses all bankers should familiarize themselves with these devious techniques. For in doing so, they will be better able to avert future losses.

Banks in every section of the country are constantly being visited by unscrupulous men and women who open accounts and then use their depositor status to perpetrate frauds against bankers and their customers.

A procedure that is popular with new-account operators is to try to alleviate suspicion by opening accounts with moderate amounts of cash. Other crooks include cash with one or more worthless checks in their deposits with the hope that the transactions will appear legitimate.

Cash Deposit Precedes Fraud

Take, for example, the case of one swindler whose habit was to open a bank account with a cash deposit of $100 or $200. On the following day, he would deposit worthless checks in amounts ranging from $1,500 to $2,500, drawn on out-of-state banks, and withdraw some of the cash used to open the account. He would then return the next day and ask the teller to inform him of the balance in his account. If the teller quoted an amount which included the large checks deposited, he would issue a check withdrawing all but a few hundred dollars. When a teller reported his balance as the amount of cash in the account exclusive of the checks, he would withdraw the cash balance and not return to the bank again.

During the period of one year, this thief earned in excess of $84,000 from his operations in ten states. His swindling career came to a halt when he was arrested by law enforcement authorities in Alexandria, Va.

The common objective of other new-account swindlers is to obtain a supply of checks with which to defraud unwary bank customers. When a swindler succeeds in obtaining a supply of checks, his next move is to withdraw the cash balance in his account. He then proceeds to pass worthless checks among merchants and others throughout the community in which he is working. Generally, this type of check swindler presents his worthless checks to his victims during non-banking hours.

Another often-used trick employed by swindlers is to open an account and later attempt a cash withdrawal by means of the split-deposit or cash-back transaction. They open bank accounts with small cash deposits and later present for deposit worthless checks written for large amounts, drawn on out-of-state banks. They consistently ask for cash back in split-deposit transactions.

Corporate Accounts Lure Crooks

Some crooks show a preference for savings accounts when laying the groundwork for their swindling operations, but checking accounts appear to be the more favored method of attack. Corporate checking accounts are frequently used as the vehicle for fraud by wily operators. For instance, one man opened an account at a bank in Virginia under the name Norfolk Iron & Steel Company. After opening the account, he passed numerous checks in the area drawn on the corporate account and totaling more than $3,500. He next appeared in the State of Iowa, where he opened an account as the

Des Moines Iron & Steel Company. This type of operator is growing in number, and is as successful today as ever, because bankers are so eager to get his business, that without verification of his claims, they proceed to process his checks.

Occasionally, reports are received from banks showing where swindlers opened accounts solely to facilitate the negotiation of stolen and forged items, such as United States Treasury checks and United States Savings Bonds.

The cases described are typical of those being reported by banks which have had experiences with new-account swindlers. All bankers should familiarize themselves with these devious techniques, for in so doing they will be better able to avert future losses to themselves, other banks, and bank customers. The check swindler's implements are new accounts, checkbooks, and passbooks. The passbook is evidence of an account and is often offered as a credential of indentification when worthless checks are presented for cashing or in a split-deposit transaction.

Ready Checks Made Crime Simple

The opportunities for worthless check writing are limited only by discretion and the number of checks in the swindler's possession. When checks and checkbooks are too easily obtained, it makes the crime all the more simple to commit.

The large volume of new accounts handled daily by some banks makes it somewhat impractical to investigate thoroughly each applicant for a personal account. A friendly but well-ordered interview should elicit answers to vital questions necessary for the bank's protection. Data concerning his former banking and business interests, as well as his present employment and address, should be verified whenever there is the slightest indication that the applicant is hesitant about furnishing the information requested.

Direct losses due to unfavorable accounts are increased by indirect losses accruing to drawee banks in connection with the handling of fraudulent items. Another appreciable expense lies in the maintenance of more or less permanent records of closed bank accounts, including those of individuals who have abused their banking privileges and are now regarded as undesirable at the banks which had previously accepted them as new customers.

In short, interviews with strangers can be instrumental in winning new friends, as well as weeding out the foes of banking. Above all, if there is any chance at all that a stranger's check might prove to be uncollectible, cash should not be given for the check or for any portion of it until it has been paid by the drawee.

New Accounts

Personal accounts, regular and special should require an initial deposit of not less than $25.00.

Business accounts should require an initial deposit of not less than $100.00.

No checks are to be given out on new accounts on the day they are opened unless okayed by an officer or branch manager, and they should never be okayed for a "first time walk in" customer.

Good Deposits

Cash, money orders, travelers' checks, cashier's checks, certified checks and loan proceeds.

If a customer insists on checks when the account is opened, you may give him checks *only* after they have been protect-o-graphed for given amounts not to exceed the total deposit.

Uncollected Funds

Checks drawn on other banks which have not been collected or paid because they are en route to the drawee for payment.

If the initial deposit is a check drawn on another bank, a three day hold should be placed on the account. If the check is drawn on an out-of-town bank, a ten day hold should be placed on the account.

Suggestions for Checking New Account Information

Information may be obtained from the following sources:

1. Telephone book.
2. Criss Cross (Haines).
3. Street Address Directory.
4. Local Directory (Chamber of Commerce).

If address and phone number are correct, this should be enough to okay opening account and mailing checks.

Order of Importance:

1. Address.
2. Phone Number.
3. Place of Employment.

Counter Checks

No counter checks will be given out unless customer is known to you or the Bookkeeping Department is called and the account is determined to be in good standing. Account numbers will be put on counter checks by bank employee.

New Account Sheet

It is extremely important that the new account form be complete and correct in every respect. If for any reason you require information on the customer at a later date, the data will be readily available.

There is no reason for not completing a new account sheet completely. If for any reason a question is left unanswered, the account should not be opened until the required information is made available to the bank either by mail or by telephone.

New Accounts—Warning Signs

1. Self employed—no phone or unlisted
2. P.O. Box—no phone or unlisted
3. Answering service, business account new
4. Minimum deposit, unemployed
5. Temporary Driver's License, Social Security card, new in area
6. No previous bank accounts
7. R.R. #, no street location
8. Living in one area, working in another, and opening the account in a third area
9. When you are unable to find the place of employment in the phone book and customer has unlisted number
10. New customer inquires about drawing against uncollected funds

CASHING CHECKS

Cashing checks is a service that most tellers perform dozens of times every business day. It is a necessary service and one that can be performed easily, quickly and accurately. However, the loss due to stolen, forged and bogus checks has increased in all areas of our country to the extent that in many locations the tellers are virtually afraid to accept any check presented, unless they know the person presenting it. To the teller, every check presented by a stranger is a potential loss. To the customer presenting the check, it is the obligation of the teller and his bank to cash it. In both instances the teller and the customer are correct. The responsibility, however, lies with the teller. It is the teller's duty to handle each and every customer as a good customer and still protect the bank from loss.

Many precautionary measures are necessary when accepting checks, and many things have been written instructing tellers on the safe-guards to be taken when cashing checks. But, nothing can replace good judgment and common sense.

Do not be afraid to ask questions about the check you are asked to cash—after all, the funds being paid out belong to the bank.

Things to Check

Every line and mark on a check has a message to tell—from the name of the bank to the kind of paper on which it is printed, and from the amount of money indicated to the signature appearing at the bottom. On all checks the teller should look for lines in the writing which are corrugated or rough along their sides. If these are detected, there is good reason to be suspicious of the check. The teller should inquire about blots, blurs, and hesitation strokes in the writing. Lines that are dark for some distance and then light might indicate that the check writer was trying to strengthen certain letters—an indication of nervousness shown by hot check artists.

The signature on personal checks should be legible. If the signature is not legible, the teller might say, "I'm sorry, but I can't read this signature, pleas spell it so I can write it below your name." Or suggest that the passer print his name below his signature. If the passer writes his initials only, ask, "Are you James C. of John C. Smith?"

If an unreadable check is presented by the maker, the teller should not hesitate to ask him to re-write it. Many checks are returned because of illegible signatures, thereby causing later expense and delay in collection. They may be uncollectible as a result.

On company payroll checks there are often spaces for more than one signature. These spaces should be filled with the signatures of authorized people. Phrases are often written on bogus checks to give them an authentic appearance such as, "for wages" "for rent." These notations give the check a "filled out" appearance, which should not be considered in arriving at its worth.

The most important consideration is to be sure that the check presented is a negotiable instrument. (See exhibit #1.)

1. Date not stale or post dated
2. Written and figure amount are the same
3. Signed by the maker
4. Must contain an order to pay and a payee
5. Drawee bank city and state

EXHIBIT #1
NEGOTIABLE INSTRUMENT

101
Sept. 1, 1975 13-31/420

PAY TO THE ORDER OF Robert G. Smith $ 21.50

Twenty One and 50/100 ------------------ DOLLARS

CB THE CITY BANK
Cincinnati, Ohio 45201

FOR ____________ Robert G. Smith

⑆0234⑈0012⑆ 149⑈33779⑈

WARNING SIGNS WHEN CASHING CHECKS

Numbered Checks

102
____________ 19__ 13-31/420

PAY TO THE ORDER OF ____________ $ ______

____________ DOLLARS

FOR ____________ ____________

After a thorough study by merchants and bankers, it was discovered that 90% of all checks returned, that became a collection problem, were numbered 200 and below. Be especially alert on checks that are numbered 101-200.

Counter Checks

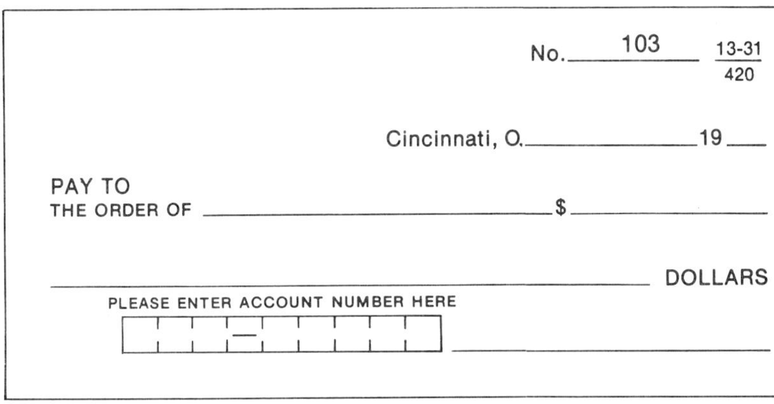
No. 103 13-31/420

Cincinnati, O. ______ 19__

PAY TO THE ORDER OF ______ $______

______ DOLLARS

PLEASE ENTER ACCOUNT NUMBER HERE

Always a problem, know your bank's account numbering system. Many checks are presented with fraudulent account numbers, especially when less cash on a deposit is involved.

Initial Issue Checks

104

13-31/420

______ 19__

PAY TO THE ORDER OF ______ $______

______ DOLLARS

FOR ______

:0234‴0012⁚ 50‴

A very dangerous check, because the customer's account number is imprinted on the check. In the case of a new account, you have no way of knowing how good or bad the account will become. Always check bookkeeping to verify balance before cashing any checks, regardless of amount.

ENDORSEMENTS

An endorsement has two primary functions. In the first place, it operates to transfer to the endorsee the title of the instrument. The title to the instrument is transferred, not merely by the holder's writing his name on the instrument, but by this act plus delivery of the instrument. Writing accompanied by delivery is the normal meaning of endorsement. In the second place, an endorsement is a promise. The endorser, in writing his name on the instrument, impliedly promises certain things about the instrument, such as its genuineness and its freedom from defenses.

Be careful about cashing checks that have more than one endorsement on them, and especially examine them for missing, defective, special, or restrictive endorsements.

Suggest to the person presenting a check that it be endorsed *exactly* as it is made out. If the person's name is misspelled or is incorrect in some way, suggest that he endorse the check twice; first exactly as his name appears on it, and second as he customarily signs his name.

Although pencil endorsements are legal, the check should be endorsed in ink or indelible pencil. Some drawers, such as Government agencies and insurance companies, may insist that endorsements on the checks be written in ink.

Become familiar with the kinds of commonly known endorsements: (1) blank endorsement, (2) special, (3) restrictive, (4) qualified, (5) conditional. A brief explanation of each follows:

(1) *Blank Endorsement:* This endorsement consists simply of the endorser's signature on the back of the check and specifies no endorsee. A payee, James B. White, would endorse thus:

James B. White

The payee must endorse exactly as his name appears on the face of the check. He may then add his customary or legal signature, such as James Barton White. The teller must be certain that the person who endorses is really James B. White.

(2) *Special Endorsement:* This endorsement specified the person to whom or to whose order the instrument is to be payable. James B. White may endorse a check made payable to him as follows:

Pay to the order of
George A. Brown
James B. White

Only George A. Brown can then negotiate the check—that is, pass title to someone else.

(3) *Restrictive Endorsement:* The endorsement restricts the rights of the endorsee, and is generally used to prevent further negotiation of the instrument. For example:

For deposit in
Blank National Bank
James B. White

The teller cannot, of course, cash such a check; it must be deposited in the Blank National Bank. Customers should be instructed to use this form of endorsement on checks which are being deposited by mail.

(4) *Qualified Endorsement:* This is an endorsement which frees the endorser from certain liabilities to subsequent holders—usually because he received no benefit from the check. The following is an example:

Pay to the order of
Blank National Bank
without recourse
James B. White

(5) *Conditional Endorsement:* The payee may endorse in the following manner:

Pay to the order of
George A. Brown
when he completes the garage
at 141 Summer Street
James B. White

An endorsement in this form does not impose upon the drawee bank the responsibility of ascertaining whether the condition has been fulfilled. If such a check is presented bearing a Conditional Endorsement, the teller should refer it to an officer.

TELLER ERRORS WHICH INCUR LOSSES

A teller is in a position where he may involve the bank in losses not only in the way of good will and business, but also financially, to a considerable extent.

The following examples of teller errors often occur.

Paying a check with a forged signature, or a check which required two or more signatures, one of which was omitted.

Certifying a check bearing a false signature.

Paying a check which has been poorly written—for a larger amount than called for.

Not noticing that the figures and written part of a check do not correspond, and paying the amount which is not written out in the body, (the legal amount).

Certifying or paying a check for which there are insufficient funds on the books or where funds have been trusteed, attached, or bankruptcy proceedings have been instituted. Similarly dissolving of partnerships may involve the freezing of funds.

Payment of checks upon which stop payments have been issued.

Paying a check upon which an endorsement has been forged or through oversight, a check which has not been endorsed or the endorsement is incomplete as for example a check requiring two endorsements.

Overlooking an item on a deposit ticket listed as cash (or not described at all), and later when a bill ticket is called for by the Proving Department—receive assurance from the customer that he enclosed the cash.

Losing count of the bills in large or involved deposits, particularly the number of hundreds.

Certifying a check which has been altered as regards the amount.

Paying a counterfeit check, or taking in counterfeit bills and silver coins.

Making a transaction which includes "splitting" a check and crediting part of it to an account.

Paying a "stale check," check which has been held by the payee an unusually long time and which may have been presumed lost.

Receiving coupons in coupon envelopes without verifying each envelope to assure the fact that contents are as described.

Cashing bonds which may prove to have been stolen or lost. The same applies to coupons.

Permitting overdrafts through being unaware of status of accounts. Many such overdrafts are eventually charged to profit and loss.

Paying check against uncollected funds.

Closing accounts and neglecting to ascertain if service charges are included.

Paying checks on account which has filed or been petitioned into bankruptcy.

Leaving items of cash in drawers at day's close of business when locking up or dropping it on floor or waste basket. .

Neglecting to keep all cash under control so that opportunity is available for theft, either from within the bank or outside.

CHECK KITING

A kite is a piece of paper, held aloft by nothing but motion and air. If one does not run fast the kite will never get off the ground, and once aloft a continuous effort is necessary or it will fall to earth immediately.

A check kite operates in the same manner. It is based on a piece of paper (a check) which moves around through much illegitimate motion, and is held up by thin air and expectations.

Check kiting is also known as "Playing the Float." It is or has been done by almost everyone. The housewife who writes a check to the grocer the day before payday, is kiting on the certain hope that it will not reach the bank before her husband can deposit his paycheck the next day and beat it there.

The Controller of a large corporation is kiting when he meets the company payroll with a large check drawn on an out of state bank where the funds will not be collected for several days.

Both of these kites are normally permitted and to a degree are considered satisfactory to the bank. The kite which poses the greatest loss problem, and which you must help to stop, is the intentional kite by the depositor in need of funds, but unable to secure a loan in the normal fashion. He sees the kite as his only source for a non-interest bearing loan.

The principal culprit in this situation could easily be a proprietor of a small sole-owner company who maintains a marginal checking account at your bank. For example, his debts exceed his receivables by $2,000.00, but he anticipates that he will be able to pay back the money in three months.

He goes to another bank, maybe in your same city, but usually about 20-50 miles away, and opens a checking account in his own name or the name of the same company that he is using at your bank. He now writes himself a check drawn on his account at the other bank for $2,000.00 and cashes it with you. He now has the money he needs to pay his bills. He must cover that check however, so he writes a check in this same amount on your bank and travels to the other bank and deposits it to his new account there.

He is operating on the knowledge that it will take two to three days for the check you cashed for him to reach the other bank for payment, and by the time it does, the check he deposited at the other bank, drawn on your bank will be there to cover it. Now, however, he has to cover the second check, so he again writes a check on the other bank and *deposits* it with you. So now the third check will cover the second check.

This game will continue as long as allowed. If you don't catch him, all he has to do is make that trip between banks every other day, depositing a check in each, drawn on the other. At such time as he is able to pay back the money, he simply inserts a cash deposit instead of a check in whichever bank his last check was written.

You may wonder what is so terrible about this, after all the banks did get paid back and no one lost any money. Think again. The bank lost interest on that money for three months. Also, what if he hadn't gotten the money to close out the kite, and pay everyone off. Then one of the banks would be out $2,000.00. Or, what if the other bank had caught on, and returned the checks drawn on them, but deposited with you as "Not Paid—Uncollected Funds." Now it's too late and your bank is out the money, because you gave him cash to start the kite. How can you stop this "kite," so that your bank does not lose money?

1. Be watchful for the customer who makes a regular

deposit every day or every other day, when that deposit consists of no cash, but just checks drawn on himself or his company at another bank, and payable to himself or his company.

2. If his bank statement looks like this:

Date	Checks	Deposits	Balance
June 3		1,800.00	2,000.00
4	2,010.00		-10.00 OD
5		2,050.00	2,040.00
6	1,900.00		140.00
7		2,100.00	2,240.00
8	1,100.00, 1,000.00		140.00
11		1,700.00	1,840.00
12	1,900.00		-60.00 OD
13		2,200.00	2,140.00
14	2,100.00		40.00
17		1,600.00	1,640.00
18	800.00, 1,000.00		-160.00 OD
19		2,400.00	2,240.00
20	2,000.00		240.00
21		1,500.00	1,740.00

Note that every other day there is a deposit to offset checks on intervening days. He will often go into overdraft status, but will cover it the next day with a big check. If you see a statement like this, your suspicion should be immediate.

It is not only a new customer, or one who has been with the bank a year or so who will do this. Anyone, including old established customers, may try this scheme if the need for quick money develops.

Bookkeepers

The bookkeepers are the persons most familiar with the individual demand deposit accounts. They should be the first persons to suspect a kite if they are aware of the indicators. Bookkeepers should be trained to look for:

1. A check and deposit on the same day of approximately the same amounts so that the resulting balance in the account does not change substantially.

2. Checks payable to the maker but deposited in another bank.

3. Large transactions, particularly in a personal account with a normally small balance.

4. Repeated checks to the same payee.

5. Any irregular or unusual transaction.

Statement Checkers

No kite should ever go unsuspected past the persons who examine the monthly statements if they are properly trained. They have before them all of the checks that have been paid by the bank during the period and the statement itself. The checks are examined for irregularities such as post or stale dates, forgery of the maker's signature, and inconsistent amounts, while the statements are examined to detect errors in posting. To inspect them for the signs of a kite would require very little additional effort. The signs that these personnel should be alert for are:

1. Continuous activity—regular deposits and withdrawals. (Generally, the average balance in the account is less than the size of the transactlon).

2. Checks payable to the maker of same payee and deposited in a different bank.

3. Checks in amounts similar to the deposits.

4. Large transactions, either checks or deposits.

5. Any unusual transaction.

Tellers

The teller is not in the position that the bookkeeper and statement checkers are to detect a kite but he should be aware of the practice and report any suspicious item or customer that meets any of the following criteria:

1. Regular deposits of checks drawn to the same person and/or drawn on the same bank.

2. Large deposits. (Particularly a deposit composed of one or a few large checks).

3. Repeated requests for information concerning customer's account.

Computer Reports

Since many banks are now on computers, reports are available to use in detecting a kite.

1. Debits in excess of available balance. This is not fool proof as most banks are on a two day float and most checks take three to ten days to clear.
2. Referred Items: all items deposited and checks over $5,000.00. Items in question can be pulled and checked to see where deposits are coming from and where checks are going.

Cash Items

Your Cash Items Clerk sees all items charged back to your customers' accounts. They are in an ideal position to watch for danger signs.

Overdraft Reports

In most cases, accounts involved in kiting eventually become overdrawn. Any accounts (business) in an overdraft condition should be checked to the last deposit for uncollected funds and where checks in file have been paid.

Monthly Service Charge

In most cases, you will receive a report that will list average balance, collected and uncollected balances. If uncollected balance is high, account should be checked carefully.

Reports from Telephone Clerks

Someone who is kiting must know if everything is working properly, and may call frequently to check balance and items that are in and paid.

Determining Potential Loss

When you are made aware of the fact that your bank is involved in a kite, it is necessary for you, at this point to determine your potential loss.

1. Place a full hold on the account involved. If you have more than one account for this customer, place holds on all accounts.

2. Obtain a statement on the account or accounts.

3. Most checks deposited will clear within ten working days.

4. Count back ten working days on statement, add the deposits from that date to present, subtract current balance. This total will be the potential loss. Have deposit tickets pulled from the file. In most cases, people that are involved in kiting will have cash on their deposit to make them look good. This cash amount may also be subtracted from the potential loss. Have photostats made of all checks deposited to the account in last ten days. Check each one with bank on which they are drawn. Some will have been paid. Those paid may be subtracted from potential loss balance.

FRAUD AND FORGERY

EMBEZZLEMENT

January 1, 1975 to June 30, 1975

	Cases	Loot
Commercial Banks	3754	$71,306,956
Savings & Loans and Mutual Savings Banks	272	$3,152,821
Credit Union	224	$864,588
Totals	4250	$75,324,365

FBI BANK CRIME STATISTICS

Perhaps one reason people tend to be tolerant of the embezzler is that they don't feel personally threatened by his transgressions. The embezzler seldom has to resort to force or violence. The victim of his purloinings is usually an impersonal, inanimate company or corporation. Thus, many people feel that, as individuals, they are in no danger from him. The average citizen doesn't consider the fact that the embezzler takes money from all of us in the form of higher prices for the products and services of industry.

Perhaps, also, some people can see something of themselves in the embezzler, and thus they may judge him leniently. The embezzler is frequently a member of the middle or upper class. Often he is college educated and has been exposed to all the ethical values that western civilization holds dear. Usually, he doesn't consider himself to be a "real criminal." He is convinced that he's just "borrowing" the money or taking something which the employers "owe" him.

But despite the sometimes benign image of the embezzler, the fact remains that he is dangerous and does serious harm to thousands of American businesses every year—to the management, to the stockholders, and to the employees of these businesses, and to the depositors in financial institutions.

The American embezzler lives in every state, in large cities and small towns. He may be employed in any business, industry or financial institution; he may be a public official. He can hold any position from company president to unlettered stock clerk. It isn't necessary that he handle money. If he has the intent to embezzle, the opportunities to put his intent into practice will present themselves to him.

How Do They Steal?

There are literally hundreds of known ways of stealing from an employer, and security experts warn that new methods or new twists in existing methods are being devised almost every day. Business thieves are extremely resourceful and will take advantage of every weakness in an employer's operations, such as unpoliced trash barrels, employee parking areas too close to receiving lots, and factory exits that aren't supervised.

At the white collar office level, pilfering of the petty cash, kiting in the accounts receivable, over-extension in cash returns, falsification of records on accounts payable, and other forms of embezzlement involving even larger losses to the employer are common. More often than not, poor supervision, bad or antiquated office procedures or bookkeeping methods and too much trust in key personnel make it all too easy for the dishonest employee to steal from the company shelves or coffers, sometimes for years without detection.

The essential difference between "white collar crime," as embezzlement is often called, and robbery or burglary, is that of trust. Unlike burglars, embezzlers are employees in positions of trust. They already have the key or the right combination. Many have access to company funds, by one means or another. They can find ways also to falsify records and cover up defalcations.

The ways of the industrial thief are manifold. Whether it is the appliance store repairman who carts new merchandise out of the store by attaching false repair tickets, the store clerk who places expensive merchandise in boxes marked for cheaper items, the sales girl who wears store clothing home under her own, or the supermarket manager who sets up his own cash register and check-out lane, the men and women who steal more than $10,000,000 a day from American business are the everyday people we all know and work with. Employee dishonesty accounts for a third of the undercover work of the famous Pinkerton Detective Agency, and it is reported that the schemes that agency uncovers can boggle the imagination.

In an article in The Wall Street Journal, a 33-year-old data processing specialist was quoted as saying, "I could steal a company blind in three months and leave its books looking balanced." He added that it is a simple matter for a crook with technical know-how and a little imagination to program a computer to fleece a company and fool its auditors. According to him, executives seldom question the reliability of financial results that come from complex million-dollar machines. "They simply forget that the machines have been built to do whatever the operators direct," he explains. "There's nothing to stop them from working quite efficiently for a crook."

Why Do They Steal?

The embezzler often seems to be a pretty nice fellow on the surface. So what makes him steal? The motive may grow out of any one of a whole range of human emotions, ambitions, difficulties and desires. The traditional causes, and those which appeal to the public's imagination—gambling, drinking, and the "other woman"—are still predominant, with drug addiction now a factor as well. But there are other less dramatic reasons, such as the expense of operating a small business on the side, the need for home improvements, or heavy medical expenses. Or, the embezzler may feel a need to get even with his employer for real or fancied wrongs.

The President's Commission on Law Enforcement and

Administration of Justice says "Corporate and business white collar crime is closely associated with a widespread notion that, when making money is involved, anything goes."

One of the chief reasons an employee will steal is that he has been living beyond his income, a fairly common practice in these days of high taxes, installment buying and large families with higher living and education costs. Another common reason is the existence of an extended illness in the family, which consumes the family savings.

Embezzlement is an insidious crime. It usually starts with small thefts and grows as the embezzler becomes bolder. Even after an employee has been caught in the act, the employer will often try to "play it down." He may be embarrassed that someone in whom he has placed his faith and confidence has taken advantage of him, or, ironically, he may pity the employee and refuse to prosecute because of his feeling for the employee or his family. Unfortunately, this attitude can encourage other employees to try their luck at dipping into the till. If a greater amount of publicity were given to embezzlements within private industry, far more employers would be aware of the serious exposure existing within their own businesses. Paradoxically, embezzlement increases in times of prosperity. Employees become over-extended for credit, loan interest notes are often higher and labor shortages prevent employers from fully checking the references of job applicants. Inflation and spiraling costs of living put increasing strain on the ability of employees to resist the temptation to embezzle.

What Can Be Done?

Security controls should be set up within your banks to protect your employees against the temptations of crime. You must ask yourself in every case of employee fraud, "Where have we gone wrong?" Did we develop enough rapport with the employee that he could come to us with his problems? Does he earn a competitive salary? Temptation and inadequate salaries are a tough combination to combat. Does he have a place to come for financial aid? You should have a plan for him to borrow money without having his personal life brought out in the open; be kind, be considerate, make him want to come back for a loan. The weakness of our employees must not be abused but taken into consideration.

Employees should be protected against the temptation to

crime—through adequate pay, through a real concern in their financial affairs, through systems and controls to shelter them from temptation and through provision of a place where they may go if they need money.

Where embezzlement is concerned, no area of an organization is beyond suspicion. Employers should institute procedures that will permit them to detect dishonest actions in any division of the firm as soon as possible. The procedures should be such that supervision and verification at all stages of an operation promptly bring to light any irregularities and lead to the detection of a dishonest employee.

It is generally good practice not to put one employee in complete charge of any one phase of administration where accounts receivable or payable are involved; for example, a credit manager should not be permitted to receive money and at the same time be in charge of posting and deposits and the preparation, mailing and distribution of monthly statements to clients.

Cashiers or accountants should prepare the reports of receipts, which should be verified by someone else who would be responsible in turn for deposits and the posting of ledgers.

Collection receipts and bank deposits should be verified as to their individual entries and not as to totals only. This should be done by someone other than the person preparing the statement. Also, the monthly itemized statement should be verified with the bank.

Spot-checks, audits, and inventories should be made at frequent intervals, and on a suprise basis, and the results compared with other results that will corroborate them or prove them in error.

Depending on the nature of the business, there should be periodic revisions of the auditing and security measures to avoid a pattern that can easily be detected and taken advantage of by dishonest employees.

Keys should not be distributed among too many of the personnel and the safe combination should be known by as few persons as possible.

CHECK FRAUDS

Unfortunately, today the bad check problem is like the weather. Everyone talks about it, but no one does anything about it.

It is reasonable to assume that for every problem facing bankers today in regard to loss due to bad checks there is an answer, a workable solution that will enable them to control a large portion of the one billion dollar annual loss suffered by themselves and merchants.

New Accounts

To better serve the community, bankers have the obligation and responsibility of opening new accounts with the same care and judgment that is taken in executing a loan.

When opening a new account it is essential that the individual opening the account have good identification. The employment, address, phone number, and all other information should be checked thoroughly for the validity of it before the initial issue of checks. It is not unusual to have an account opened with a small cash deposit and within several weeks find that hundreds of dollars in worthless checks have been passed. In most cases when these new account sheets are checked, most or all of the information is incorrect. Needless to say these losses should never have occurred.

Counter Checks

Counter checks in all cases should be removed from bank lobbies, and given out only by your new accounts personnel, and then only after a call to your bookkeeping section to verify the standing of the account. In addition to this measure the customer's account number should be placed on the check by the bank employee. This simple procedure can eliminate loss to merchants and yourself.

In some cases local merchants require the bank to furnish blank checks for their customers' convenience. In these cases, require the company to stamp their name on the payee line of each check. It would then be the company's responsibility for those checks cashed.

Exchange of Information

All bankers are aware of the undesirable customer that goes from bank to bank. When one bank closes his account for return check charges or kiting he simply goes to another bank and trouble starts anew. If banks could be convinced to exchange information on bad accounts, the floaters would soon be out of business and everyone concerned would save time and money.

Stolen Checks

Without question the most severe loss to merchants is stolen or forged checks. Here again the banks can be of help by forming security councils. Basically, the councils are designed to cooperate on a hot line, seek enactment of bad check laws, educate cashiers and clerks to bad check pitfalls, and encourage the demand for more and better identification from those writing checks.

The most successful of these has been the hot line. It is an expanded version of a round robin warning service most police departments have operated for years.

Of course the most essential thing is cooperation from banks, merchants, and local law enforcement agencies, all of whom are usually more than willing to participate in a program of this type.

CONTROLLING CREDIT CARD FRAUD

The Franklin National Bank of Long Island, New York, is generally credited with being the first bank in this country to adopt credit cards. From this auspicious beginning, the bank credit card monster has grown to a point where most banks are afraid not to issue their own card, either individually or through a franchise arrangement with one or both of the two major card systems, BankAmericard or MasterCharge.

Bank credit cards have been a boon to customers, and in most cases bank profits as well. The fly in the ointment has been that they are also a boon to the nation's criminal element.

Because they were a new phenomenon which far outdistanced the legal statutes concerning fraudulent use, the initial reaction of police and the courts was generally negative. The principal feeling was, and to a large degree still is, "If the banks want to issue those things, they deserve to get stuck."

State and Federal lawmakers, after much pressure by the banking and retail industry, finally passed laws regarding the fraudulent possession and use of credit cards, but the police still consider credit card investigations to be fruitless and the courts, when forced to handle prosecution, do it with a surprising degree of leniency.

Fraudulent possession and use of credit cards have provided vital evidence in investigations of robbery, burglary, and even kidnapping and murder, and because of these factors, we can hopefully envision the day when law enforcement personnel will actively assist in the investigation of credit card crimes.

For the time being however, the banks who are in the credit card business must be willing to accept the losses from fraud, or be willing to pay the cost of their own credit card security personnel to attempt to hold down these losses.

The following comments, which we believe are the most concise and meaningful on the subject of credit card fraud control are from a speech by Mr. Samuel E. Bray, Director of Security, Town and Country Charge, Continental Illinois National Bank, delivered to an Ohio Bankers Association Security Seminar in 1970.

The control of fraud is a demanding, full-time occupation. The security of a credit card operation cannot be assigned to an amateur as an additional duty, or to a Sunday afternoon armchair detective. The practice of security is a professional art demanding trained practitioners and a knowledgeable management.

Each card-issuing bank must protect its investment in such an operation by doing everything in its power to protect that system. In this context the security representative's job is educational as well as protective, since security in these areas is a total concept.

When we speak of credit card protection, we are speaking of security from the time the negative is used to produce the printing plates through the moment when the card leaves the physical control of bank representatives and enters the U.S. mails. If the job is properly done, innumerable problems will be eliminated before they have a chance to appear. As a point of reference, the minimum standards published by Interbank are an excellent guide to security in the manufacturing phase. It should be continually borne in mind, however, that there are *minimum* standards. No document can hope to provide for all contingencies or to cover the needs peculiar to individual charge card issuers. Charge plates which have reached the stage in manufacture where they are usable by fraud-oriented persons are literally "money on the loose." It has been our experience that such a card may be worth as much as five thousand dollars in the hands of a professional passer. A card, therefore, becomes a dangerous piece of material when its face format has been completed and it is completely printed. It becomes doubly dangerous when the embossing process has been completed.

Because of these factors and because of the inherent value of uncontrolled cards, positive steps should be taken to see that all operations are controlled to the fullest extent possible. This entails physical counts of finished blank plastics delivered for processing and a check against manufacturers' invoices on a per-card basis.

When security is satisfied that counts tally, all blanks should be secured in a vault and all plastics to be embossed should be signed out, again on an individual count basis to the individual embossing operator. At the end of each shift, finished cards plus unused and spoiled cards should be collected and tallied against the number issued to the individual operator. All tallies should coincide and any discrepancies should be explained. In embossing operations involving the author's bank, the embossing operation is isolated and all employees are required to change into work smocks which are surrendered at the end of a working shift. Wherever possible, separate vaults should be maintained for each operation.

The stuffing of cards into mailers should take place immediately after the finished plastics are issued for that purpose. All such stuffing should be under the immediate supervision of a competent supervisor and a physical inspection of finished mailers should be undertaken prior to placing them in mail sacks or other bulk containers. Again, this count should tally with the number of cards issued to the mailing section for processing. To reiterate: it should be physically verified that cards are in the mailers before they are placed in mailing containers.

Prior to mailing, the cooperation of the postal authorities should be solicited, and from them high theft and problem areas should be ascertained by zip code zones. Mailing into these critical zip code areas should be by registered mail only. All other mailings should be zip code sorted—first class mail dropped at post offices with low crime rate experiences. It will be found that the Postal Inspection service will be more than glad to cooperate in securing a safe route for these mailings.

One final word on preparation and mailing. The envelope is *not* the place to advertise the credit card system. Such statements as "Here is your new 'Instant Money' credit card" on the exterior of an envelope can wipe out all the careful efforts at control which have been exercised up to the point of mailing. These envelopes should show the customer's name and address, and the return address of the sender—nothing else. Neither should the charge account number be displayed anywhere where it can be seen from the outside of the carrier.

Once a secure mailing has been accomplished, internal controls must be reviewed and a chain of responsibility established for IBM print-outs bearing name and account numbers, unused plastics, and other sensitive items. Such materials should be placed in secured vaults, controlled by responsible custodians and should be distributed on a strict "need to know/need to handle" basis.

Finally, a consistent policy of handling detected fraud cases is essential for a secure charge card system. Since most issuing agencies are now members of Interbank or similar national and international systems, credit cards have become attractive to the organized, sophisticated criminal societies. Because of this, it must be clearly established that banks will vigorously investigate and prosecute any attempt to misuse their systems. In this area, a clear understanding of the principles involved and a respect for the need for such activities is essential on the part of bank management. This is an educational process which is one of the security officer's biggest jobs and which heavily influences the responses of police and prosecuting officers upon whom the success of the system rests.

If the authorities are aware that they are dealing with professional, competent security representatives, and know that complaining banks are prepared to follow through with apprehension and prosecution of fraud artists and others, you may depend on their full cooperation in the control of credit card abuse. Nothing does more damage to the security system than the bank which institutes investigation and apprehension, and then declines prosecution at the last moment because restitution has been made. Attitudes such as these quickly become known in the law enforcement community and the next complaint made by such a group is met with polite disinterest. The result is a license to steal for anyone who wishes to take advantage of the situation.

There is a further educational job for the security man. It entails the continuing training of the merchant who handles such cards and the customer who uses them.

Far too many merchants will accept credit cards without ever checking to see that the signature on the back and the one on the receipt match. It is almost certain that some businessmen have no idea what the back of a credit card looks like. The merchant must be made aware of the significance of floor limits, heavy buying of salable items, the skipping of an individual from division to division within a store, or from check-out desk to check-out desk, and other questionable activities by individuals using credit cards.

At the same time, the customer must be made aware that the credit card represents actual money. He must be made to know that the card should be in his control at all times, properly signed, and he should require that the merchant be sure that the card is properly used. A $5,000 bill illustrates the value of a single, conveniently-handled credit card. We would not dream of placing a $5,000 bill in the glove compartment of our auto or leaving it on the table at home, yet this is what is done in too many cases with the credit card.

In summary, three concepts are basic to a secure credit card industry—continued vigilance in their preparation and control, a vigorous policy of detection and prosecution where they are abused, and a comprehensive program of education for bank officials, merchants and the public.

Credit Card Department Check List

In all areas of banking there is a loss potential, but in the credit card business, being the newest segment of banking, far less security is known or practiced than in other phases of banking.

The following is a check list that may be utilized for the prevention of credit card fraud.

1. Institute a continuing program of audit verification of card holder balances
2. Clearly define who has the authority to re-age accounts, increase card holders limits, change addresses, and issue new cards
3. Know who is permitted to change billing dates and issue refunds for service charges, etc.
4. Know how many employees have part time jobs and why, last time you ran a security or credit check on employees
5. Check friends of employees that are past due on their payments
6. Check your shipments and mailings of cards handled, and who has access to new cards
7. Check to see if you are mailing cards registered or certified to doubtful neighborhoods
8. Institute a system of card recovery from merchants, after pick up of cards on hot card list or from undesirable customers who are over their limit or past due on payments

9. Check companies that have an excess of card holder refunds or that have the habit of accepting sales on stolen cards

10. Have someone who checks card activity for sales abuse

11. Have one person responsible for contacting customers to go over their credit limit

12. Check for multiple sales on same merchant on same customer accounts.

FORGERY LOSSES

A given individual armed only with a ball-point pen and a piece of paper can create more havoc than the desperado armed with lethal weapons. Of the three main avenues of assault to which banks are subject, the attack by the holdup man has the greatest emotional impact, the attack by the embezzler shocks our sensibilities the most because it is an inside job, and the attack by the so-called "paper-hanger," who cleverly persuades us to exchange cash for worthless scraps of paper, strangely enough, hits us hardest in the pocketbook.

The holdup is the most sensational and grabs the headlines. Indeed, the increase in this type of attack aroused public and congressional opinion to the extent that special legislation was adopted—The Bank Protection Act of 1968. Nevertheless, the monetary cost of holdups is considerably less than the other two methods of attack. Holdups in 1975 resulted in net losses of $17.5 million. By contrast losses due to embezzlement amounted to $75.3 million in 1975. There seems to be no question, however, that losses due to bad check artists and bank credit card operators exceed the losses involved in holdups and embezzlements. Check losses in 1975 were estimated at $3 billion and bank credit card losses at $460 million.

The bad check operator comes in two varieties—the amateur who is a nuisance but not too costly, and the professional who is clever, resourceful and well-prepared, who operates in groups or rings and who plays for big stakes. The bank that has not been victimized by this type of character is lucky because these crooks know their business and they frequently take even the most careful tellers, platform people and officers.

They are extremely well organized, and they have two main sources of raw material—genuine or genuine-looking blank checks. In the first place, they can make their own and many of these rings own or are associated with small and not too conscientious printing shops. But, lacking such an association, they simply steal printed MICR encoded checks, either from the printing supply houses or from the office, store or factory of the depositor.

14 Offices in One Day—Net Loss $8,400

A Philadelphia National Bank a few years ago experienced an incident involving instruments produced by a collaborating printer. A young man came into the bank and purchased a money order for $700. This young man was a cat's paw for a ring, since the master-minds seldom expose themselves to capture. In this case, the ring supplied a fair amount of capital—$700 in cash. Nothing happened for 10 days, during which time the money order was turned over to a printer who was purportedly located in Cleveland, Ohio. At a later date the young man hit 14 offices in one day, cashing beautiful reproductions of the original $700 money order. The net loss was $8,400. One branch manager hesitated because of the size of the money order. He took the phony item and compared it with blank money orders in stock. The reproduction was so perfect that as a result of this comparison he was convinced the instrument was genuine.

"That's My Signature. . . I Think"

In another case, a check drawn by a local savings and loan association aroused suspicion. . .unfortunately after it had been cashed. It wasn't the instrument itself that rang a bell, but apparently someone thought the check-casher looked like a known bad check artist. As a precautionary measure the check was sent over to the savings and loan association and shown to the man who had ostensibly signed it. He pronounced it as genuine; and the fraud was not discovered until, during processing, it developed that the original bearing the same number as the phony item had already been paid.

Stealing pre-printed, pre-encoded checks goes on with disturbing frequency. A legitimate printer, during a run of checks, discovered some malfunction. He stopped the press, repaired the damage and started the run over again. He failed to see to it that the checks produced through the first abortive run were destroyed. One of his employees carried them away that night and in due course a number of them were successfully cashed.

A bank in Philadelphia received 8,000 pre-encoded printed checks which were to be picked up by a local hospital. While waiting for a messenger from the hospital, the 8,000 checks disappeared. Subsequently, 5,000 were found in the basement of the bank in a trash can; 3,000 found their way into the hands of a well-organized ring. Many of them were successfully negotiated. In some cases, to allay suspicion, one of the check passers, who was a woman, appeared at the teller's window in a stiffly-starched, gleaming white nurse's uniform! What an appropriate uniform to wear while cashing, ostensibly, a hospital paycheck.

Now that we have given you some examples of how good the adversaries are, let us give you some examples of how lax and careless we in the banking and finance industry are becoming. First of all, do you remember the days when we used to examine signatures? In the case of most stolen checks, the crooks have no idea of the identity of the authorized signer, but the fact is that they can use almost any name and get away with it! Checks that should be signed by a Brown, Smith or White are signed by a Mr. Bogolofsky, but nobody notices the difference! In fact, each one of us can probably cite instances from the experience of our own banks where pre-printed and pre-encoded paychecks bearing no signature at all were honored without question.

Not long ago a customer approached one of our platform officers and announced that his office had been burglarized and his checkbook stolen. The platform officer, gave him good advice: "We will close the old account, transfer the balance according to your records to a new account bearing a new number and then we will be safe." The customer did as he was told and was surprised at the end of the month to find literally dozens of the old, stolen checks enclosed with his bank statement. What happened was an example of a bank service beyond the call of duty. Since the original account had been closed, the checks were rejected by the computer, as is normal, and were delivered to a desk clerk for special handling. This particular clerk was familiar with the name of the company and was surprised to learn that the account apparently had been closed. She looked it up in the files and found that the account was still on our books and immediately arrived at what was to her an inescapable conclusion! Some dumb printer had misencoded the checks using the wrong account number! So she proceeded to correct the account number, attached an override to the checks and forced the checks through for posting to the new account.

Insurance? Forget It!

There can be no question that our metropolitan banks, at least, are being hurt and hurt rather badly, both by the professional and amateur "paperhanger." The question is, "What do we do about it?" It seems that there are only three alternatives: 1) We can insure against these losses; 2) we can self-insure and absorb the losses; 3) we can take some sensible loss prevention measures.

As far as insurance is concerned, sound advice is to forget it... except for the really catastrophic loss. Let's face the facts; as far as insurance against fraud losses is concerned, banks are poor risks, and the record certainly is not getting any better. Many insurance companies will no longer write bankers blanket bond insurance. Those that do are insisting on higher and higher deductibles, particularly for metropolitan banks. Most banks in this country with assets in excess of $1 billion have been forced to accept a $100,000 deductible clause. Those in this class whose three-year contracts will shortly come up for renewal will have difficulty obtaining a lower deductible...assuming that they can afford the premium! A $100,000 deductible will force the insured bank to absorb about 99 per cent of the incidents of loss and a very substantial proportion of the dollar amount. Therefor, as far as insurance is concerned, we would advise you (and your insurance carrier will probably tell you in more forceful terms) that you should accept a high deductible clause with as much good grace as you can muster, because, actually, you have no choice in the matter. It is essential that you do nothing to disturb your real catastrophe coverage. In fact, be forewarned, that if things keep on, insurance may be all but impossible to obtain. Self-insurance without a sound program of loss prevention would invite disaster.

How does one establish a loss prevention program? It appears that the place to start is at the main points of exposure—the new account desk and the teller's window.

New Account Desk Is Vulnerable

A captured crook once boasted that if he could get by the new account desk of any bank, the success of his plans was practically assured. We are convinced that some banks have no idea of the degree of exposure involved in routine activity of accepting new accounts. As you all know, identification is not an exact science, and it is not too difficult for an imposter to open an account in other than his rightful name. We take particular pains to record information, residence, place of employment, previous bank accounts, etc., concerning the new depositor but we do nothing about it. Numerous times banks have first suffered a loss and then proceeded to call the employer listed in an attempt to learn the whereabouts of the conniving depositor...only to discover that the alleged employer never heard of the man. A single telephone call at the time the account was opened might have saved $400 or $500.

Just for fun, take a look at the information you obtain when a person comes in to make a $200 installment loan. Most banks obtain detailed financial information and check the names through a credit rating bureau. Compare that with the minimal information you obtain when you open a new account and consider the fact that most of us do not even check these few facts. It is relatively easy to open a special checking account or savings account and give as your address a vacant lot, garage or gas station, as well as a fictitious employer.

Now consider the risk involved in these two transactions. Your maximum loss in the $200 loan is $200, if the borrower skips and never makes a payment! But now compute the maximum potential loss in opening a new account! We can't say that it is unlimited, but, it could reach astronomical proportions. When we open a new account, we engage to guarantee our depositor's endorsement on any and all financial instruments that he submits to us for collection. Even if the items are paid, our exposure on our warranties runs for three years under the Uniform Commercial Code. It appears doubtless that the exposure to fraud in opening a $10 special checking account is far greater than the exposure in granting a modest installment loan! Why, then, are we so careless in one instance and so careful in the other?

The answer to this is more careful selection and training of all platform personnel and particularly those assigned to the duty of opening new accounts.

Teller Has Been "Set Up" For a Fall

The next line of defense is the teller. We find it difficult to criticize the teller when he has been "set up" by the new account desk. But the tellers, undoubtedly, play a big role in the mounting frauds perpetrated on banks by bad check artists. This is primarily a personnel problem. It is difficult to obtain and retain qualified tellers; but we are convinced, on the other hand, that additional efforts must be taken to properly train the employee who pays out money over a window.

We also find it difficult to criticize tellers who have not been given sufficient time for training and seasoning. We often wonder whether management fully appreciates the tremendous responsibilities it unhesitatingly delegates to very young people who, in our opinion, perform far better than we can have any reason to hope, but who can hardly be expected to be a match for the mature, seasoned, professional crooks with whom they are constantly confronted. We should not be too surprised if forged credentials, stolen checks, fraudulent use of legitimate accounts, worthless deposits, split deposits and all the other tricks in the "paperhanger's" bag are successful most of the time.

This is the price we pay for rapid expansion. All metropolitan financial institutions are rapidly expanding and establishing branches. How often are these expansion plans logically and realistically restrained by the personnel development plans? How much more important is the establishment of a branch than the ability of a bank or savings & loan to provide competent and capable personnel? An expansion-minded management might consider the inevitable losses that result from the failure of personnel development programs to keep pace as a calculated risk. Perhaps so, but common sense dictates a very careful look at the amount of realized losses to determine if the prize is worth the price.

IDENTIFICATION

The matter of identification is important, not only from the standpoint of the teller, but also that of the customer himself.

A teller will from time to time encounter unusual idiosyncrasies of human nature. The most baffling of all is the antagonism aroused by the simplest and most ordinary of all requests, that of asking for identification. Experience seems to have shown that in many cases the annoyance has root in the manner in which the request was submitted.

A teller is naturally on guard when a stranger presents a check for encashment, and frequently his attitude, tone of voice or facial expression betrays the fact and transmits the message quicker and clearer than any words he might utter. The inner reaction of the customer is automatic. "This man thinks I am irregular—a thief—a crook preying on bank employees." Invariably resentment follows.

The teller's responsibility not only includes an obligation to the bank in safeguarding its funds, but also that the account and business matters of the customer be guarded and kept confidential. It is to the customer's advantage that unauthorized persons are not permitted access to information or opportunity to tamper with his account through fraud or deceit. The bank's liability and the responsibility of the teller extends not only beyond the cashing of checks and drafts but to the delivery of statements and other information which might be sought with a view toward fraud or furthering breaches of trust. A so-called "poker face" attitude (with a smile) and altogether impersonal mien coupled with a polite remark that the stranger's face is not familiar, has he an account at this particular office of the bank, followed by the statement that identification is a requisite in transactions of this type, has been determined as the most satisfactory procedure.

"Have you got something with your name on it?" A remark often heard at tellers' windows, is inadequate.

Invariably the customer is confused, and he proceeds to draw forth a mountain of documents from his pockets or wallet, spreading them around and frequently dropping them on the floor or leaving one or two on the wicket ledge as he departs.

If the customer exhibits indecision relative to the type of identification a teller desires to see, a good assist is to ask for an automobile license or registration, charge cards at the large stores, or any of the various I.D. cards issued by manufacturing concerns, government agencies or military discharge photostat cards. Considerable difficulty is encountered by the submittal of Social Security cards and the now recognized fact that they offer inadequate identification because of the ease with which fraudulent cards of this type are obtained. These cards should never be accepted as complete identification.

In the cashing of Welfare or government checks strangely enough a teller encounters no end of difficulty. People on welfare are often sensitive and misinterpret a request for identification as an attempt at prying into their business, particularly as regards their qualifying as a welfare recipient.

Similarly government checks even though they clearly bear the imprint, "Require Identification" bring forth the remark from the payee, "it's a government check, isn't it? Don't you think the U.S. Government is financially responsible?"

Tact and patience is the only answer to this problem, and of course the answer is that "We are trying to protect you, sir (or madam)." Many of these checks are lost in the mail and appear months later having been cashed in different cities. Quietly pointing out that the identification is a protective measure instituted at least partially for the payee's benefit has been found helpful in soothing ruffled feelings many times. Forged and stolen identification has always and will continue to be a problem. Numerous cases of fraud by this method are reported each year.

If a teller exercises every precaution and a doubt still lingers in his mind, the only course left is to share the responsibility with an official and suggest that the check be O.K.'d or initialed by the office manager or cashier.

A point specially stressed in all conversation with a customer regarding identification is to shy away entirely from the word "stolen" or any intimation along that line. Whether the customer is a thief or not, the reaction to such suggestions is one of anger, reproach and loud talking. The teller wants to avoid this.

Value of Identification

1. Excellent
    a. Office or shop picture ID with description
2. Good
    a. Office or shop picture ID with description
    b. Your state driver's license (if not stolen) with photograph
    c. Armed forces or dependent ID card with photograph
    d. State or County photograph welfare ID card
3. Fair
    a. Insurance card, Blue Cross
    b. Company pass, no picture
    c. Courtesy card
    d. Credit card
    e. Passport
4. Poor
    a. Social Security card

b. Lodge card
c. Out of state driver's license
d. Fishing or hunting license
e. Letter from maker of check

Ask yourself these questions:

1. Does the identification really belong to the person presenting it?
2. Does the check appear to be genuine and unaltered?
3. Is the appearance of the endorser consistent with the kind of person who would be expected to have such identification?

Anyone cashing a government check should compare the purpose for which the check is drawn, which is stated on the face of the check, with the person presenting it. For instance, a 14-year-old boy should not be cashing an Old Age and Survivor's Insurance check.

DO Make a notation on the back of a check as to the nature of the identification accepted in cases where you require identification.

Be especially careful about securing satisfactory identification when you are asked to cash Government checks. Because of the large volume of Government checks issued and the delay necessarily involved in paying them, utmost caution should be used when cashing them.

Remember that any credentials ordinarily offered for identification purposes may easily be fraudulently duplicated. They may also be obtained by deceit or ruse, by payment of a fee, by finding, or by theft.

Become acquainted with methods followed in defrauding banks through use of forged officer's initials. A bank officer should not return an initialed check with the person for whom it was approved; but, instead, such a check should be given directly to the teller or guard.

Remember that *"Strangers are not always crooks, but crooks are usually strangers."* A bank's obligations and responsibilities are to its depositors. Services to others are in the nature of courtesy accommodations.

Become familiar with the booklet "Identification With and

Without Credentials" published by the Insurance and Protective Committee of The American Bankers Association.

DON'T Place complete reliance on the credentials usually offered for identification purposes. Social Security cards should never be accepted as identification for they are easily obtained and it is common practice for mail thieves to use them. Automobile operator's and chauffeur's licenses which appear to be the favored type of identification should be carefully examined, for the impressions of the validating stamp of the issuing office may have been forged or counterfeited. Also, many licensees fail to sign their licenses.

Permit the apparent genuineness of an instrument to lessen the care taken in identifying the purported owner.

CHECKS, FOREIGN

DO Become familiar with your policy concerning cashing checks drawn against Canadian or other foreign funds; your policy relating to cashing foreign checks against U.S. dollars should also be ascertained.

CHECKS, IRREGULAR FORM

DO Scrutinize carefully, before payment, checks written on counter check forms, blank forms, or on forms of other banks with the drawee bank's name changed. Many checks bearing forged signatures appear in this form.

CHECKS, CORPORATION

DON'T Cash checks that are made payable to a corporation; such checks should be deposited in the corporation's own account unless a corporate resolution authorizes otherwise.

ILLEGIBLE FIGURES

DO Write in pencil, in a clear space, the correct amount on checks that are badly scrawled, smudged, or otherwise illegible on their face.

FRAUD

DO Be on the lookout for checks that differ in appearance or design from those that are normally used by your customers. If you have any doubt about any check presented to you, refer it to an officer.

DON'T Let a personal friendship interfere with your sense of fairness and integrity. Being a "good fellow" doesn't require a teller to overlook or cover up seemingly innocent but not strictly on-the-level dealings of close friends or fellow employees.

MONEY ORDERS, POSTAL

DO Become familiar with the current system for handling postal money orders. Postal money orders are issued at all post offices and may be cashed at any post office or bank within a period of one year. They are cleared in the same way as checks.

Be certain before cashing or accepting a money order that it is correctly endorsed and that the person presenting it is properly identified.

DON'T Cash a postal money order which is presented for payment more than one year later than the last day of the month in which it was issued.

Cash or accept for deposit a postal money order bearing an alteration or erasure because this renders the order void.

Cash a postal money order for a person other than the payee or the endorser. The payee must endorse the money order on the line marked "Payee" and if he transfers it to any other person or firm he must insert that name on the line marked "Pay To". More than one endorsement is prohibited by law. Bank endorsement stamps are not regarded as endorsements in the case of postal money orders.

CHECKS, TRAVELER'S

DO Make certain that all traveler's checks which you cash are countersigned in your presence.

Refer to an officer any form of traveler's check with which you are not familiar.

COUNTERFEITING

Counterfeiting of money is one of the oldest crimes in history. At some periods of early history, it was considered treasonous and was punishable by death.

During the American Revolution, the British counterfeited our currency in such large amounts that the Continental currency soon became worthless. "Not worth a Continental"—a phrase expressing worthlessness—became a popular expression still heard today.

It was estimated that about one-third of all the currency in circulation was counterfeit at the time of the Civil War. The genuine paper currency in circulation was printed by many banks in hundreds of different designs until a National currency was adopted in 1863. Even the National currency was counterfeited.

The situation was critical, therefore, the Government established the United States Secret Service on July 5, 1865, to suppress the wide-spread counterfeiting of the Nation's currency. Although the counterfeiting of money was substantially suppressed after the establishment of the Secret Service, it is still a problem and represents a potential danger to the Nation's economy.

Today, counterfeiting once again is on the rise. A reason for this is the ease and speed with which large quantities of counterfeit currency can be produced using modern photographic and print equipment. Therefore, we must guard against this threat and one way to do this is by being more familiar with our currency and know how to detect a counterfeit.

COUNTERFEIT BILLS

The best method of detecting a counterfeit note is to compare it with a genuine note of the same denomination and series.

1. Rubbing a bill on a piece of paper will not prove it is genuine or counterfeit: ink can be rubbed from good bills as well as bad ones.
2. Know your money—Study the bills you receive, so as to become familiar with the workmanship on them. Knowing the standard features of genuine paper currency of the United

States is the most important step in detecting and identifying counterfeit notes.

If available, use a small magnifying glass and look for the red and blue fibers in the paper. Sometimes counterfeiters attempt to copy these fibers by printing colored lines on the paper.

If the note that you question does contain these fibers then, next, compare its other features with the genuine note. *Look for differences—not similarities.*

The counterfeiter does not have access to equipment as sophisticated as the Government's; therefore, his notes are inferior. Most counterfeits are made by a photo-mechanical process. The printing appears flat and lacks the three-dimensional quality of genuine notes.

Further, many of the delicate lines in the portrait of a counterfeit note are broken and often are missing. The lines in the portrait background, if you look closely, form squares and on counterfeits some of these squares are often filled in.

PORTRAIT AND BACKGROUND

Genuine

Lifelike appearance; delicate lines are sharp and distinct; background lines are regular and unbroken.

Counterfeit

Does it appear flat and dull? Are the shading lines broken or missing? Are the background lines ragged?

Facts About United States Currency

There are three types of U.S. paper currency in circulation. The name of each type note appears on the upper face of the note. The different type notes are further identified by the color of their Treasury Seal and Serial Numbers.

Type	Treasury Seal and Serial Number	Denomination
Federal Reserve Notes	Green	$1, $5, $10 $20, $50, $100
United States Notes	Red	$2 and $5
Silver Certificates	Blue	$1, $5, and $10

*Silver Certificates are no longer being printed.

*The $100 Federal Reserve Note is the highest denomination note *now* being printed.

*Genuine currency is printed on special paper manufactured under strict Government control.

*The paper contains many small red and blue fibers visible to the naked eye.

*Genuine notes are printed from engraved plates by master craftsmen who use the most sophisticated equipment.

Positions of Important Features of Paper Currency

	Genuine	Counterfeit
Treasury Seal	Clear and distinct; sawtooth points are sharp and even.	Is it printed in the right color? Are the design elements clear and distinct? Are the points ragged?
Serial Numbers	Distinctive style; serial numbers evenly spaced and aligned.	Are they printed in the right color? Are the numbers poorly spaced or not aligned?

Very simply stated, good money is good because it is made from special materials, with special equipment, by craftsmen at the Bureau of Engraving and Printing. In any basic examination of genuine currency we must consider three factors: (1) paper, (2) ink, and (3) the printing technique involved.

The paper is 100% rag content paper, containing very distinctive red and blue fibers interspersed throughout. This paper is manufactured by a private paper firm under contract to the Treasury Department. Security at the plant is maintained by Treasury Department personnel and the production is subject to strict daily audit. Federal regulations prohibit commercial products in similitude in this country.

The ink used in printing genuine currency is manufactured at the Bureau of Engraving and Printing. The formula is unique and is maintained in absolute secrecy within the department.

In addition to the special paper and unique formula ink, a third and equally important security feature of genuine currency is that it is printed from plates executed by the world's most skilled craftsmen using the world's most sophisticated equipment.

Two high quality types of printing are used in printing genuine currency—*Intaglio* and *Typographic.*

The basic note is printed by the Intaglio process. In Intaglio printing the ink lies in the recesses of the plate and is picked up by the paper.

The changeable features on the face of the note are printed by the typographic printing process—that is, the Treasury Seal, serial numbers, series, signatures of the Secretary and Treasurer, and in the case of Federal Reserve notes, the Federal Reserve Bank Seal and the four bank identification numbers. In typographic printing, the ink lies on the top of the plate and is transferred to the paper by pressure—similar in effect to a typewriter key hitting the paper. In the printing trade, typographic printing is sometimes referred to as letterpress or relief.

Now let us detail how the counterfeiter makes his note. More than 95% of all counterfeits made today are manufactured by what is normally referred to as the "Offset Printing Process."

In order to print a counterfeit note, the counterfeiter first must obtain all the necessary supplies. This means going to printing supply houses, photographic shops, ink suppliers, paper houses, etc., until he accumulates exactly what he needs to begin his work.

The first step in his actual operation is usually the making of a photographic negative from a genuine note. The counterfeiter usually obtains a new, unhandled genuine note from a bank so that he can obtain a negative as free from defects as possible. The counterfeiter often retouches certain portions of his work which are not up to his standard or quality. He may take portions from several different negatives and piece them together.

He produces a plate by placing the negative in contact with a pre-sensitized plate; that is, a plate containing a coating which is sensitive to a light source. After exposure, the plate is developed and he is ready to print. The counterfeiter often makes maximum use of his plate, making 3 or 4 impressions on one plate.

Since the seal and serial number are printed in a different color than the balance of the face impression on all genuine currency, the counterfeiter must make at least one separate plate to print these features. He again usually makes maximum use of the plate.

With all the confidence of any skilled artist, he then proceeds to run off his notes—with the same ease he might use in printing the office news letter. Using any tool at his disposal, he then cuts his product to note size and is ready to start on a passing spree.

Based upon experience with this type of offender, we generally classify the counterfeiter into one of three groups, (1) the professional criminal, (2) the print shop owner who decides to compete with the Bureau of Engraving and Printing, and (3) the employee in a commercial printing shop who uses his employer's equipment and supplies, without the owner's knowledge, and manufactures counterfeit notes.

The professional criminal usually operates in an organized manner. Mr. "Big" might be one or more top-drawer criminals, who handles vice, gambling, and other criminal endeavors and decides to enter the counterfeiting scene. He will hire a printer who might be on the fringe of the rackets to make the notes and quickly pays him off. He will then turn over the distribution of the notes to a "Lieutenant" who will distribute the notes throughout the country through his normal criminal contacts, i.e., fences, burglars, prostitutes. Mr. "Big" might ask 10% for the product; the area distributor will raise the price to about 25%, and the local distributor might sell to the passer for as high as 35%. The apprehension of the passer in this type of operation is only a step toward finding and arresting Mr. "Big."

The Secret Service concentrates heavily upon this type of operation, since this particular group represents the greatest threat to the Nation's economy because of its ability to spread many counterfeits over a large area in a short space of time.

The second type of counterfeiter is the small print shop owner who decides he just can't make a profit through his normal legitimate business dealings and competes with Uncle Sam. He usually takes pride in his product and makes a fairly deceptive note. Since he lacks the normal criminal contacts, his area of distribution is necessarily confined. The important factor to this investigation is that when arrested, a passer in this type of operation usually reveals the manufacturer. It naturally follows that this type of operation represents less of a threat to the Nation's economy than the previous group, since it lacks the nation-wide distribution outlets.

The third type of counterfeiter is the employee in the print shop. He usually tells his boss that he would like to work late at night, or on weekends, to complete some job for the firm. When he is alone, he makes his plates and prints the notes using company supplies and equipment. This again represents a particular type of counterfeiter, who although much less professional, is nonetheless as potentially threatening. The distribution of his bills will be more limited; the actions of the passer more naive and, the likelihood of his apprehension in proximity to his shop is much greater.

Counterfeiting is a risky, and not always lucrative practice. An example is the man who worked for over a year perfecting a very special technique of printing with the result that he produced the most deceptive counterfeit $20 note seen in over 25 years. He operated successfully for about two years, traveling across the country about five times with one accomplice passing the notes in small towns and large cities. He was arrested in Seattle, and his accomplice in Kansas City. Secret Service agents found $17,000 in the notes secreted inside the paneling of the door and behind the motor of the automatic windows. He and his friend received long prison sentences and an analysis of their profits discloses that they averaged about $1,520 per year—not even up to the minimum wage.

COUNTERFEIT COINS

Compare—Suspected counterfeit coin with genuine coin of the same denomination.

Feel—Many counterfeit coins seem greasy.

Corrugated Outer Edge—Genuine coins (10 cents, 25 cents, 50 cents and $1.00) have an even and distinct reeding (corrugated outer edge). The reeding on counterfeits is uneven, crooked and oftentimes missing. A band of copper should also be clearly visible on genuine 10 cent and 25 cent pieces struck on the new *non-silver* clad alloys. These coins bear dates of 1965 and later.

Cut Edges—Genuine coins are not easily cut with a knife. Counterfeits are often easily cut or bent under slight pressure.

Acid Test—Acid will blacken a scraped or cut portion of most counterfeit coins but will not discolor genuine *silver* coins (all 50 cent coins and 10 cent and 25 cent pieces bearing dates prior to 1965).

Formula—(Acid test for *silver* coins only)
Silver nitrate . . . . 10 gr.
Nitric acid . . . . 1 cc.
Distilled water . . . . 30 cc.
This solution can be bought for a few cents in any drugstore.

COUNTERFEIT CHECKS

Since 1968, numerous counterfeit checks have appeared and many losses have been incurred. However, in a careful study we find that there are certain tell-tale signs that appear on the majority of the bogus checks, regardless of the companies that appear on the check.

Listed below, are five of those signs that appear on about 90% of the fraudulent checks.

1. Magnetic encoding same color as colors on checks

2. Magnetic encoding not in proper location; usually higher than normal
3. Information on check incorrect; bank address, etc.
4. Typed payee rather than computer printing
5. Other imperfections, in many cases poor typing

SWINDLES

TELEGRAPH SWINDLES

The telegraph swindle is perpetrated with and without credentials of identification. Purposely, the swindler places himself at a distance from the drawee bank so that the use of the telegraph as a means of effecting a payment of funds appears justified. The use of telegraphic codes between banks causes this type of swindler to select a location where there is no bank and a telegraphic order to pay cash can be executed only through a telegraph office or hotel. It is generally accepted that where a bank complies with a telegraphic request for funds, whether the sender is a customer or merely poses as a customer, and the bank wires money to be paid upon identification, the telegraph company is not liable for payment to an impostor provided that the company uses proper care. In cases of this kind, it should be recognized that credentials may be displayed for identification with which the personnel of a telegraph office could hardly be expected to be familiar. Other factors entering into the transfer of funds by telegraph are delayed discovery of error or fraud, if any, and the matter of furnishing witnesses when a telegraph swindle is the basis for criminal prosecution. Court action in some cases involves time and transportation charges and incidentals of witnesses, the total of which is often considered prohibitive to prosecution.

For the transfer of funds by telegraph, the use of the A.B.A. code between member banks has been helpful in frustrating telegraph swindles.

USES AND ABUSES OF THE TELEPHONE

The telephone is a hapless accomplice of swindlers when used for purposes for which it was not intended. It has been used and doubtless will continue to be used to displace credentials of identification presented in person. The advance telephone call received by a banker on behalf of a swindler is made by a banker on invitation or suggestion of a swindler to identify him as the payee of a worthless check. It is a frame-up in which the banker unwittingly plays into an act pre-staged for him. Likewise, the telephone call by banker to broker or broker to banker when made under circumstances prearranged by the swindler or an accomplice, usually leads to a misunderstanding and the banker or broker becoming the victim of a check fraud.

Decoy Telephone Calls

The more successful fraudulent schemes are modeled along the line of common practices between depositors and their banks. One much favored by check swindlers is the fake telephone call made in the name of a compnay to the effect that their Mr. John Q. Walton is on his way to the bank and when he arrives please tell him to call the office. Upon being given the message, Mr. John Q. Walton immediately telephones and for an effect intended for the banker, a brief conversation takes place. He then presents a check ostensibly drawn by the company named and too often it is cashed without question.

The advance telephone call acquaints the banker with the name of the man, links him with the company and the check, and leads to the belief that identification has been established. The smart payee, on his part, always has in readiness some plausible explanation of his title to the check. At another bank a swindler, pretending to have telephoned a depositor under similar circumstances, presented a check ostensibly signed by that depositor and commented that it was in payment of his car which he had just sold to the depositor.

In another job by two swindlers, one called on a medical doctor on a pretext of wanting a treatment, but instead he wanted to study the doctor's voice so that he could imitate it. An accomplice appeared at the doctor's bank with a check to be cashed and suggested that the banker telephone the doctor to verify the item. Before the call could be made, the banker received a telephone call by a man who said he was the doctor and that he had sent a man over with a $300 check to be cashed. The banker was satisfied that the voice was that of the doctor and cashed the check. When it was returned unpaid, the banker learned that the doctor had not telephoned.

PIGEON DROP

The pigeon drop is a swindle by confidence artists, against customers of the bank. It most often involves elderly customers, and while it causes no loss of bank funds, it does harm the bank's reputation in the community, and almost always costs the loss of a customer.

The victims, while giving away their money on the strength of a "something for nothing" scheme, will almost always hold the bank, and you, responsible for letting them have their own money to give away in the first place.

The bank's reputation is damaged by newspaper headlines which usually read "Elderly Woman Swindled of $5,000, Which She Got at (Your) Bank."

There are two general themes to the pigeon drop. In the first place, the elderly victim is approached on the street by a stranger, who asks for directions, or begins some type of innocous conversation. During the course of the resulting friendly chat, a second stranger appears, who tells both that she has just found an unmarked package containing a large sum of money. She allows both the victim and the first stranger to see it. She states that she is new in town, and does not know what to do with the money.

The first stranger identifies herself as an employee of some type professional man (such as a doctor or lawyer). She suggests that they call her employer and ask him what to do. After this phony phone call, she returns to state that he suggests they all divide up the money.

The finder now asks the victim (in this case, an elderly woman) and the other stranger to put up some evidence of "Good Faith," to show that if either of them had been the finder, they would have shared the money with her. Both agree to do so, and go to their respective banks to draw out some money. Of course only the victim actually draws out the money. She will approach you and hand in a withdrawal slip for a large amount. She will want it in cash, and want you to place it in a plain envelope. Then she will return with it to meet the others at a pre-arranged point.

While showing them the money, one will distract her attention while the other switches envelopes. They will hand her back an envelope containing cut newspaper, and tell her to redeposit it in the bank, and then meet them to split the found money. As soon as she heads for the bank, they disappear with her funds, and she does not realize she's been swindled until she gives you the cut paper to put back in her account.

The second scheme involves the phony bank examiner. An elderly customer receives a phone call from a man identifying himself as a Bank Examiner, involved in checking your bank. He asks the customer if she banks with you, and if told yes, he wants her to let him verify her account.

He tries to get her to tell him her balance, and surprisingly most people will have no hesitation about discussing their accounts if they think the caller has some official standing (Examiner, FBI Agent, Police Detective).

After ascertaining that the victim has enough money to make it worthwhile, the phony examiner explains that one of the tellers in the bank is embezzling money, and he wants the customer to help catch the teller. The customer agrees to do this.

The phony bank examiner tells her to go to the bank and withdraw most of her money. She is to get it in cash, and have the teller put it in a plain envelope. She is then to bring it outside the bank, to where he will meet her. He will either take the money and give her a receipt or tell her that he just wants to look at the money, after which she can return to the bank and redeposit it.

In either case, the switch will be made and she will never see the money or the phony examiner again.

To stop this type of fraud, you must be alert to customers, generally elderly, who wish to withdraw a large amount from their account, who want it in cash, and who want you to put the money in an envelope for them. Whenever you are faced with this situation, try to get the customer to take a cashier's check instead of cash. Most customers needing funds for legitimate purposes will accept a cashier's check. The elderly victim of these schemes will not readily accept a check because she has been told that she must have cash to either "show good faith" or for examination to help catch the embezzling teller.

If the customer refuses the cashier's check and demands cash, refer her to your bank manager. Advise him you think this may be a pigeon drop. By calm questioning, he may be able to determine what is happening, and dissuade the customer from giving her money away.

Suggested questions to ask customer: Has anyone presented themselves to you as an FBI agent, bank examiner, police officer, detective or bank official, and requested any information about your account, or asked you to withdraw any amount from your account, whether to help them "catch someone" or to show "good faith?"

SNEAK THEFTS

Sneak thefts have been determined, for the most part, as crimes of opportunity, crimes made possible principally by the thoughtlessness of bank tellers rather than carelessness.

A study made by one of the better known Insurance and Protective Agencies of this type of loss suffered by bank tellers has revealed that thefts of this nature are not always planned in their entirety by the thieves and their accomplices but occur by circumstance and opportunity provided by a teller or an assistant in the teller's cage.

Contributory negligence on the part of the teller, providing accessibility to the loot during banking hours, and the fact that this type of loss always occurs during the regular banking hours, would appear to be the chief aids to sneak thieves as they ply their trade. Successful thefts depend largely upon three factors within a bank. First, currency or securities exposed to view inside a teller's cage; second, fixtures that permit access to currency or securities, with or without the use of a stick, rod or cane; and third, telephone calls by which tellers or other personnel can be lured away from the scene.

The first factor is present in many banks because deposits, withdrawals, payrolls or delivery of securities come at unusual times. The second is most important because inaccessibility of currency defeats the plan of thieves. Some banks have added to the equipment of tellers cages an opaque plate, which covers the entire wicket. When the teller leaves his cage the plate is put in place so that the contents of the cage are out of sight of thieves.

The third factor pertaining to communication facilities that favor the sneak thief is often remedied by installing a telephone in each teller's cage, or between each set of two cages, and so arranged that it can be used while the teller continues to face the wicket. This eliminates entirely the teller being required to leave his cage if called upon to comply with a customer's phone request.

Where sneak thieves operate in teams of two or more, one is assigned to make the telephone call from a station outside the bank, or to engage the guard or nearby teller in conversation to divert attention away from his accomplice who is striking the target by lifting cash or securities left exposed.

A teller can offer a helpful service in this regard if he notes persons loitering suspiciously in the bank, usually strangers, by calling them to the attention of a guard or official. Also they may note briefly in writing or mentally, strangers applying to open checking accounts or savings accounts with checks drawn on out of town banks or with little cash. It is by such methods that thieves obtain information of the bank premises and names of officers and tellers for later use in sneak thefts. It affords them an opportunity to gain time within the bank to lay out their plans and strategy.

The most outstanding loss due to a sneak theft recently reported occurred in New York. A sneak theft of $75,000 occurred after a teller had "sacked" five and ten dollar bills in that amount, placed the bag with two other bags of currency, for pickup by armored-truck guards and gone to lunch. Later the guards arrived and in the company of another teller went to the cage for the pickup. Two bags of currency were there, but the bag containing the $75,000 was missing. All three bags were described as representing merely "a routine shipment of surplus currency," and were placed upon a shelf in the teller's cage near the rear door of the bank.

After an investigation uncovered no clues, police concluded that since the lobby was crowded with lines of people in front of all teller's windows, someone unnoticed had made his way to the currency bags and also unnoticed succeeded in making his way out the rear door.

Another bank reported recently that a sealed money bag containing $3,000 in bills disappeared from a teller's cage. The money had been delivered by armored truck and signed for by the teller.

A few minutes after delivery of the bag the teller was called to answer the telephone in another teller's cage at the extreme end of the bank. Before leaving his cage he placed the bag on a counter distant from the wicket—but several minutes later when he returned the bag was gone.

Tellers should be doubly careful, cautious and watchful regarding cash which is open to view of the public. Under no circumstances should it be left thus exposed when one is not in the cage.

FLIM FLAMS

This is another name for the scheme used by the "Short Change

Artist." He obtains the bank's money with your consent, but without your knowledge.

He approaches your window in an obvious hurry, and hands you a stack of mixed denomination bills, generally three 20's, two 10's and four 5's. He asks for two 50's in exchange. While you are counting the money he gave you, and ensuring that it totals $100.00, he talks continually, telling how he is in a great hurry, and how you are the slowest teller he has ever seen.

Just as you hand him the two 50's, he changes his mind, and hands you back one of them. He asks for two 20's and a 10 instead. As you reach for these, he stops you and asks for the 50 back. He will then ask you for the two 20's and the ten as well. If you give them to him, he now has $50 of the bank's money.

Reading the account, you will say that it can't happen to you. It is too simple to work, and you are to smart to fall for this trick. However, the thing he has going for him is that running line of chatter about his big hurry and your slowness. He never stops. He wants to keep your mind off counting that money, and he has been so successful in the past with other tellers, that he knows the scheme works.

If you appear particularly sharp, he will throw in a few additional passes until he realizes that you can't be flim-flammed, and then he will take his original $100, and wander off to the next bank, where the next teller may not be as sharp.

The way to defeat this operator is to never allow yourself to be hurried, and concentrate on each transaction. Do not allow anyone who says you are a slow or poor teller to get under your skin. Take your time and be right.

A second method of flim-flam involves the customer who comes to your window and says he is a collector, who is looking for a certain type of bill, generally a $50, bearing the Federal Reserve District letter "P" on the seal. He asks you to look at all your $50's and see if you can find one for him. You will not be able to find one (as there is no Federal Reserve District with the letter "P"), but he will offer to help you look. Don't hand this man any money so he can help you, or you will never see it again.

The schemes of this nature are as many and varied as the minds of men who can make them, so you must always be on the alert.

One other scheme bears mentioning because unlike the other two which are pulled by strangers, this one is most often pulled by a customer of the bank.

A customer, not necessarily known to you by name, approaches your window and presents a deposit ticket with a cash deposit. You will accept the deposit, and validate the ticket. The customer will watch to see if you look at the customer copy before you hand it back. If not, the customer will accept it and leave the bank. In a few hours, the customer will return and show you an unvalidated customer copy of the deposit ticket and ask you to note that the validation did not come through on his copy. If you still have the original ticket in your work, and compare the two, you will find that they compare exactly, except for the validation. The customer now asks you to validate his copy for his records.

Unbeknownst to you, when the customer prepared the original deposit he used two carbon tickets, so the impressions would be the same. He saved one and presented you the other with the deposit. His first customer copy was validated, but he hoped you would not look to check this fact before handing it back, and you did not.

The customer receipt he now has given you is the copy of the second ticket, with the original teller portion torn off. If you validate this second copy for him, he will walk away a happy man. Then in about 10 days when he receives his bank statement which fails to show two deposits for the same amount, he will come in to see the bank manager, clutching both validated copies, and will claim the extra deposit, which the bank must give him because he has the evidence. Any claim on your part as to what really happened may be met by protests of innocence on his part, the veiled suggestion that you stole the money, and tore up the other deposit ticket, and lastly the hint of a civil suit against the bank.

COLLECTION OF BAD DEBTS

The principal bad debts occurring to a bank involve late or defaulted payments on installment, mortgage and commercial loans, as well as credit card charges.

With the exception of the credit card charges, most of the loans in the other three areas are secured with collateral which is either held by the bank, can be seized by foreclosure, or can be repossessed and sold.

In the cases of unsecured loans, or a remainder due after repossession and sale of the collateral, the bank must initiate collection action. Most banks maintain a unit of collection specialists to follow and recover on debts of this nature.

With the advent of bank credit cards, a new type of bad debt was forthcoming. There was no property for collateral, and the customer often had no accounts with the bank containing funds for off-set. This led in most cases to the establishment of a collection unit to handle these accounts.

Another area of consideration is the loss resulting from unjust enrichment, non-sufficient checks, and service charges from overdrawn charged off accounts. The customers in this last area are ones that are usually not pursued, aside from a telephone call and possibly a form letter requesting payment. A great opportunity for recovery is missed, for failure to use the same aggressive collection techniques in this area, as are normally used by the loan and credit card collection specialists.

A satisfactory solution to the entire problem can be obtained by the formation of a unified collection department to handle all forms of bank debts owing to the bank.

You will find in many cases that the customer who is overdue on his installment loan is also delinquent on his credit card payments, has been kiting or writing NSF checks and his checking account is probably overdrawn. By unified collection procedures, one collector can be assigned to collect the combination of all debts from one customer, without wasted effort or duplicated motion.

All persons who incur debt fall into one of four categories:

1. The customer with both the desire and the ability to repay the debt. We don't have to worry about this customer. He is the banker's profit-maker.

2. The customer who has the desire to pay, but due to circumstances which have overtaken him, he no longer has the ability to pay. This person, will probably pay the debt if given enough time, along with a little push occasionally so that he knows you are still interested in collecting. He needs minimal, non-aggressive contact on a continuing basis.

3. The customer with the ability to pay, but no desire to do so. This one must be aggressively pushed and continually contacted. The least let up by the collector will be interpreted as an opportunity to "forget all about it."

4. The customer who has neither the ability or the desire to pay. This is the familiar "dead beat." He should never have been approved for credit in the first place, and in the majority of instances, would not have become indebted to the bank

without an error in fact or in judgment by some bank employee.

The "deadbeat" is not a hopeless case, but he is close to it. All stops must be pulled out when dealing with this character. The bank must continually contact him and remind him of his fiscal responsibility and the legal ramifications if he does not do so.

IMPORTANT FACTS ABOUT PAST DUE ACCOUNTS. Every Day Past Due Accounts Remain On Your Books, They Decrease In Value. Eventually They Become Worthless!!!

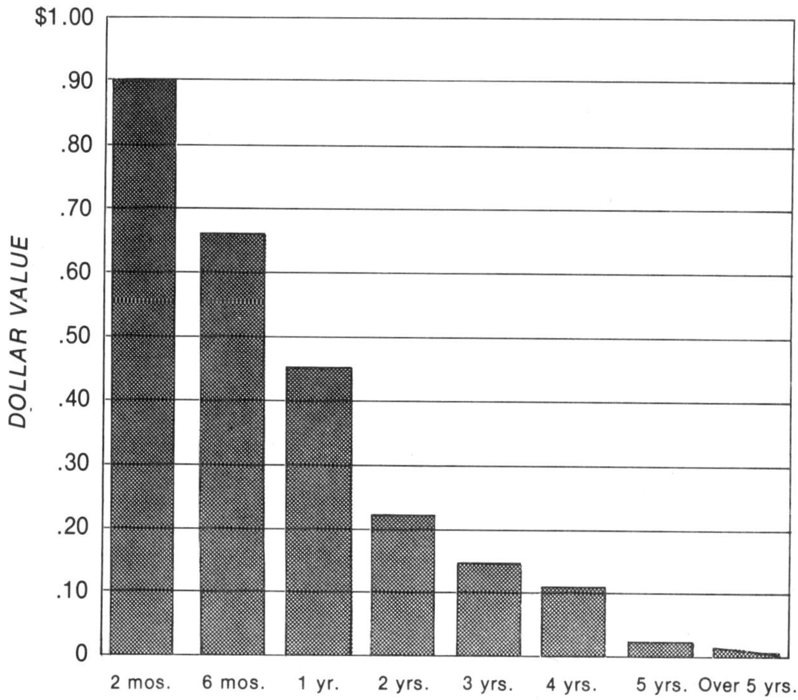

THE DECISION TO PROSECUTE

Bank robbers and burglars, counterfeiters and kidnappers are prosecuted for their crimes. The banker has no say in this matter. He expects it as a fact of life and is normally quite pleased that this is the case.

The con man who defrauds him, however, whether with bad checks, sneak thefts, forgeries, embezzlements, or kites or credit cards will often go free to attack again. This is because the banker doesn't want to get involved.

In order to prosecute, the banker must assemble the facts, arrange for personnel to go to court and testify, and pay them while there. In addition to this, his legal counsel has frightened him to death with fear of a false arrest suit wherever he initiates an arrest and prosecution.

In the long run, officials of financial institutions view it as much easier to take the loss and hope the thief will go somewhere else. We have even reached a point where embezzlers are no longer prosecuted, unless the amount stolen is sufficiently large. We terminate the small embezzler and call it "failure to follow work rules" on his employment record.

However, the banker should not be allowed to shoulder all of the blame for the failure to prosecute the criminals. He sees the court system release the thief on bond to attack again within 24 hours of his arrest. The court appearances, requiring his employees allowance of time off take days instead of hours. If and when the thief is convicted, he is placed on probation and returned to the streets to ply his trade. The thief is probably ordered to make restitution to the bank for the amount stolen, but this is never enforced, and the banker has a slim chance of recovering a cent.

If this is the case, why prosecute? The answer is survival. Although the system of criminal justice works to the thief's advantage, the banker, by prosecuting, has caused some inconvenience to the thief. He has let the thief know that the bank will not accept this state of affairs. To do nothing is to gain nothing.

When anyone steals from your bank or savings and loan—prosecute him. It is not a guarantee that he will never steal from you again, but, it is highly likely that this will be the result. You owe it to your bank to help him make the decision.

Your local police department will be most happy to cooperate in the investigation and arrest, as soon as they realize that you have adopted a principle of prosecution. A note of warning however: once you have initiated prosecution, and the arrest has been made, the thief will probably contact you, either in person or through his attorney. He will offer to pay you back the loss, if you will drop the charges against him. *DO NOT DO THIS.*

First, if you should do as he requests, you may lay your bank open to a false arrest suit. Secondly, the police who investigated the case and made the arrest will become extremely hostile. After about two or three incidents of this nature, the standing of your bank with your local police department will be zero, and they will never again voluntarily assist you to prosecute anyone.

When the thief (or his attorney) calls you regarding restitution, advise them that you would be most pleased to accept it, but that you will not drop the charge against him. Say instead, that you will be more than happy to advise the judge, at his next hearing, that he has paid back the loss, and then leave the decision regarding the charges up to the judge.

PROTECTION DURING CRISIS

BANK ROBBERY

January 1, 1975 to June 30, 1975	
Commercial Banks	1,590
Mutual Savings Banks	103
Savings and Loan Companies	480
Credit Unions	30
Total	2,203
Loot Obtained	$17,448,913
Injuries During Robberies	126
Deaths During Robberies	15
Hostages Taken	54

FBI BANK CRIME STATISTICS

Bank robbers come in all shapes, sizes and ages, and their methods of robbery follow no fixed plan. However, most robbers will commit their crime in one of the following three basic methods.

THE NOTE PASSER

This man will approach your window and try to make his crime look like a normal banking transaction. He will generally have prepared the hold-up note on the back of a bank form at one of the customer counters in the lobby. The note will read something like this: "This is a stickup. Don't hit the alarm. Give me all your big bills. I have a gun and will use it."

Irrespective of his last sentence stating that he has a gun, you may very well rest assured that he does not have any type of weapon. This man is a con artist. He knows that if he is caught in the commission of this crime and doesn't have a weapon on him, he cannot be sentenced to the penitentiary for nearly as long as the armed robber. In fact with sentencing procedures these days, his sentence will be up to ten years less than the armed robber. He is therefore taking a gamble in a game of conning you out of the money against a short prison term if caught.

Because of this, he cannot let anyone in the bank know that he is robbing the bank except the teller whom he initially approaches. Since he has no weapon and cannot defend himself, he is at your mercy. If you should, for example, faint as soon as you read the note, he must leave the bank. He cannot very well leave your window and move to a different teller after you have fallen to the floor, with the resultant confusion.

THE LONE ARMED ROBBER

This man (or woman) will approach your window and exhibit some type of weapon. He may point a gun at you. If he is shy, he will probably show you a gun stuck in the waistband of his trousers, but not take it out. He may hold up a bottle of clear liquid and say that it is nitroglycerine or acid, or he may show a stick or cylinder and claim it is dynamite or a bomb. He will orally demand the money and tell you exactly what he wants you to do. Since he is armed with a weapon, or at least appears to be, you must do what this man demands. He also would prefer that you be the only teller in the bank who knows it is being robbed, but that is only because it makes it easier to control the situation.

Each bank has certain instructions as a guide to follow. In the event any of the following suggestions conflict with instructions issued by your bank, you should follow those issued by your employer.

The instructions for dealing with the lone bandit (note passer or armed robber) are different from those dealing with the armed gang, so let us take the lone bandit first.

VICTIM TELLER

Remember that in this situation you may well be the only person in the bank who knows that it is being robbed. Therefore you have the most to remember and do to assist in the ultimate capture and conviction of the robber.

1. As soon as you realize that you have a robber at your window *activate the holdup alarm.* This action, if performed the first thing, will not arouse the bandit. He is unfamiliar with your work area and does not know where your alarm device is located or how it is activated. Do this, and then go for the money. By activating the alarm you do two things. You summon help (the police) silently, and if your bank is equipped with photographic surveillance cameras, you turn on the cameras, so that a group of photographs will be taken of the robber.

2. Open the working cash drawer in your cage, and begin to give the robber the money. Be sure that in the first handful of money you pass him is included the "Bait Money." Hopefully, you maintain a quantity of "Bait Money" which is marked. Also, if you keep this money separate and held together with a paper clip, remove the clip before you mix it in with the first handful of money you give the robber. After you have given him this first handful of money, continue to hand him money from your working cash drawer (as slowly as possible) until one of two things happen. First, when this bandit entered your bank he gave himself a specific period of time in which to commit the robbery and make his escape (normally two minutes). He also had to assume that you activated the silent alarm and that the police are responding. If his time runs out before you have emptied your teller drawer, he will turn and leave your window and you can stop handing out money. Second, when you have given him all the money in the drawer and he is still standing there looking at you, STOP and look back at him. Put an expression on your face which says, "Well, what do you want me to do now?" *DO NOT VOLUNTEER TO ROB THE BANK FOR HIM.* If he wants more money, make him ask for it. Don't say such things as "That's all the money I have in this drawer, do you want me to get my bulk currency for you" or "Do you want me to rob all the other tellers for you" or "Should I get the manager to open the vault currency chest and get you some money from there?" Remember, you want to get this man out of the bank as soon as possible. By offering him more money, you are not only increasing the loss to the bank, you are holding him in the bank. On the other hand, if this man knows more currency is available from any of these sources and demands that you get it, do so.

3. The time during which you are handing him the money will be

your only chance to look at this man, to be able to describe him, and to later recognize him. Don't look at the money. Don't look at the gun, if he has one, *LOOK AT HIM.* Determine these things: What race is he?, What height is he?, How old is he?, How much does he weigh? After you have these things firmly in your mind, try to note some other points concerning his description: What color hair, and how is it worn? What color eyes? Shape of his face? How is he dressed? (This includes color and style of clothing as well as material) What type of jewelry is he wearing? Voice and accent characteristics? These items are his description. In addition, you must look for items of recognition, because *description changes.* If this man can make a successful getaway, he will probably change his hair color and style. If he wore a beard and/or mustache, it will be shaved off. If not worn, he will try to grow one before his apprehension by police. I will guarantee you that the clothing he is wearing will be thrown away or burned. He will try to change his appearance so that you will have a difficult time ever recognizing him again. Therefore, you must be able to also look for something which he cannot change. This is where scars and marks come in. Almost everyone has some type of facial scar or blemish. Also, most people have scars on their hands, and many have prominent tatoos. So look for these things, and find at least two of them to remember him by.

4. He has now completed his robbery, and he turns from your window and walks quickly to the door. As he does this, you should hit the holdup alarm again, back out of your window and begin to walk behind the teller counter and toward the lobby in the direction of the same door through which he exited. As soon you are sure he is out of the door, let everyone in the bank know that it has been robbed. The best way to do this is to scream as loud as you can the word "ROBBERY." Continue into the lobby and go to the door through which the bandit exited. Do not attempt to follow him, but at least peer outside the door and see if you can still see him on the street. If so, stay in this position, and watch him until you can no longer see him. You may see him get in a car. If so, see if you can get the make, model, color, and license number of the car. More bank robbers are caught by a license number obtained by an alert witness, than by any other means.

5. As soon as the robber disappears from your sight, come back into the bank, and go to the nearest phone. Call the police, or the sheriff and tell him what happened. Tell him your name (Sally Smith) your position (teller); your location (the ______) what happened (I

was robbed) and now describe the man, as well as where you last saw him (a white male, about 35, six feet tall, medium build, brown hair, worn long, a mustache and small beard, wearing sunglasses, dressed in a white shirt, dark trousers, a dark blue nylon windbreaker, and wearing a red hunting cap, armed with a pistol, and I last saw him running west on Main Street and then he turned the corner south on State Street) *You and only you can make this call.* You do not have time to pass this information on to anyone else to make the call for you. The police need this information immediately. They know there is a problem at the bank because you hit the silent alarm, but they do not know what type of problem or who they are supposed to be looking for. You must tell them. When you have completed the call, *let the police hang up first.* They will have to have the information correct, and they will probably need to have you repeat certain items again, before they have a clear picture of what happened. You can hang up after they do so.

6. Now return to your window, stand in the same position you did when the robber confronted you and THINK, "What did he do?" You must protect any physical evidence the robber left behind, so try to recall what he touched, handled or dropped. Assuming he touched your deal plate, take a large piece of paper and cover it to protect any latent fingerprints. He may have had a newspaper over his hand to hide the gun from everyone but you, and he probably left this behind. Pick it up by the edges and set it behind the counter to give to the police when they arrive. Let's back up a minute to the beginning and say we are dealing with a note passer. The smart ones will show you the note, but they will never let you get hold of it, for they know it has their handwriting and latent fingerprints all over it. The amateurs, however, will actually hand you the note. If you get possession of it, read it and then let it drop to the floor behind your counter. If you were able to do this, now is the time to pick it up from the floor and set it behind your window to give to the police.

7. Now is the time to make written notes of what you remember. Write down the description of the robber in as complete detail as possible. Do not discuss your ideas with other bank employees or customers before doing this, or you will find yourself changing your mind about certain points to agree with theirs. Write down what the robber said and what his physical actions were during the robbery. Now you are through until the police arrive to question you.

You will note that at no time have you been instructed to stop and talk to anyone from the moment the robber turned and fled from your window. This is very important. Remember, as was said before, you are probably the only person in the bank who knew a robbery occurred. You let everyone else know when you screamed "Robbery," but they certainly don't need to know the details until after the initial police action has taken place. So don't take the time to let anyone get you in a conversation until after you have completed step number 7. Above all, realize that when the robber left your window, your window (and hopefully the whole bank) was closed. Do not wait on any more customers.

When you screamed "Robbery," as you ran after the robber, this was a signal to everyone else that they now had certain functions to perform to assist the police. This is what they should do:

MANAGER (or Senior Floor Officer)

The manager should leave his desk immediately and follow or meet you at the door where the robber exited. Peer out of the door and attempt to see which way the robber is going. Point him out to the manager, who then follows the robber at a discreet distance, and trys to get the description of the getaway car, and its license number. He then returns to the bank, and gives this information to the police, whom you by this time have on the telephone.

ASSISTANT MANAGER (or Head Teller)

The next Senior Officer or Head Teller should meet you and the manager at the door. He will bring the keys to the door, and after the manager leaves to follow the bandit, and you have come back inside to make the telephone call, he locks the door and remains there. He can let the manager back in on his return, and keep other persons (including customers) out. Lastly, he shall let the police know that the robber has left, and let them into the bank. He continues to remain at the door to control the exit and entrance of everyone, until the police have completed their investigation.

TELLERS

The other tellers, when they hear you yell "Robbery," close their windows and lock up their teller trucks (or drawers). If they are waiting on a customer at the time, they complete this one transaction and then close. They then announce to the customers in their area words to this effect. "We appear to have had a robbery. I don't know anymore about it than you do, but the police should be arriving in a few minutes. Would you all remain in the bank until the police arrive." At this point, there will be some customers who will want to leave the bank. If so, then the other tellers should insure that their names, addresses and telephone numbers are obtained and listed so that the police may contact them later. After all customers are identified, then the tellers should go back through their cashed checks and deposit tickets for the five minutes preceding the robbery and list all their customers, with names, addresses and telephone numbers, if available. This list is compiled and given to the police upon their arrival. This is done because these customers have been outside the bank before and during the robbery. While they were unaware that a robbery was taking place, they may have noticed something which would be of value to the police, without realizing the value of what they observed. (For example, a car with driver, and engine running parked a block from the bank).

SECRETARY (or Clerk or Bookkeeper)

This section applies to the person who answers the telephone in the course of their regular duties. After you have activated the silent holdup alarm, the police will undoubtedly call the bank to try and determine if it is a real or false alarm. The person who answers the telephone will be advised of the fact that the alarm has sounded, and be asked if there is any trouble. In as much as the robber may still be standing at the victim teller's window, she must be very cautious in how she handles the situation.

She should *never* jump up and look frantically about the bank. She should never ask out loud "Did someone hit the holdup alarm?" or "Are we being robbed?" Instead, she should calmly look over the lobby area to see if anything looks unusual. If so, she answers "I think so." On the other hand if everything looks normal, she can say "I don't think so but I will check with the manager." After talking to the manager, a decision can be made whether to report the alarm as false. Of course, if by this time the teller has screamed the word "Robbery," she can tell the police that a robbery has occurred and they should come to the bank as soon as possible.

After the call from the police, calls will come in from the press and from depositors and the general public, all of whom are anxious to know what happened. The secretary should know that it is of utmost necessity to keep the telephone lines clear for the use of the police in calling to and from the bank. She therefore must refuse at this time to talk to the press or allow them to talk to anyone in the bank. She is more courteous with depositors but cuts them off as quickly as possible, and those calls from the general public should also be ended courteously but abruptly. She tells callers the approximate time the bank will re-open for business, (generally one hour after the police have arrived and begun their investigation) and advises the press that they can speak to the manager (or other designated bank officials) at that time.

These instructions generally cover all personnel in the bank who will become involved in some phase of the robbery investigation. In addition, let us discuss the dealings with the news media following a robbery.

A bank robbery is a very newsworthy event for the local press, radio and television media. They will generally send reporters to the bank as soon as possible. The reporters will attempt to enter the bank while the police are there conducting their investigation. It is not a good idea to allow the press to enter during this phase of the investigation. The police need the time to quickly make plans to apprehend the bandit. The press does not need this time and will only hamper the conduct of the investigation by tying up persons the police need to interview. If you are questioned by anyone who is not a law enforcement officer, refuse to answer his questions and refer him to the manager.

After the police have departed, if your bank allows you to talk to the media, be cautious in how you answer their questions. Do not disclose any information about the amount of money given the bandit, or that you gave him bait money, and what it is. Give your address and phone number as that of the bank where you work. Your home address and phone number, appearing in the newspaper or over the air, will many times subject you to harassment by strangers at a later date. Do not give detailed information regarding what you did or the robber did during the robbery. A published report of your words and actions may cause you anguish when used by a defense attorney against your testimony at the trial of the robber months later.

With the exception of suggestions for dealing with news

media, the foregoing instructions apply to robberies committed by a lone person, whether armed or not. The following instructions should be followed in the event of an attack by the armed gang.

THE ARMED GANG

When the door bursts open and the masked bandits enter, they will point guns at you, and generally demand that you back away from the teller counter, or get down on the floor. They are trying to shock you so that you will do this immediately without thinking.

They do not want anyone to activate the hold-up alarm, but for the first ten seconds they are in the bank, it is impossible for them to take control of the situation unless you let them. Even though they may have cased the bank before entering, they are unsure of several things, such as how many employees are there in the bank; where are they; who is at lunch or in the back room; how many customers there are and where they are located. The bandits must assimilate this information as they look over and search thru the bank after entry. In order to do this they cannot keep their eyes on everyone at the same time.

For your own protection, you must try to activate the alarm. If the bandit is looking right at you, you cannot do this, but while he is looking at you, he is not looking at your fellow employee who therefore, has the chance to hit the alarm. On the other hand, if you have all followed the bandit's demand to "Hit the Floor," as soon as he shouted it, everyone lost the chance. So try to stay as calm as possible in those first few seconds, and hit the alarm if you have the opportunity.

After that, do exactly what the bandits say. First, put your hands up, palm out, and keep them there. This shows the robber that you offer him no threat of overt action. Then continue to face him for as long as you are standing. If he says to get on the floor, kneel down and then lay face down on the floor, and stay that way. Do not try any heriocs, such as "sneaking a look" or getting to the alarm button. Stay down and out of the way, until you hear them go out of the door.

These robbers will get the money themselves. They want you out of the way, because you impede their action. When they have left, and you get up, you will see that the back of the teller line looks like a cyclone hit it. Drawers will be thrown open, adding machines on the floor, paper bank forms and some currency will be scattered all over the place. DO NOT TRY TO TIDY UP before the police arrive. Leave everything just as it is, and get out from behind the counter and into the lobby with the customers.

The Manager should go to the door and look to see if he can see the bandits making their escape. He should return and make the phone call to the police, giving them all the facts available.

The Assistant Manager should go to the door, lock it, and stay there to control exit and entrance, and to let the police into the bank.

Each teller should hit the holdup alarm, as soon as they get off the floor, and just prior to getting out from behind the the teller counter. They then will proceed to gather the customers together in the lobby and take down names, addresses, and phone numbers for the police. They also may try to recall names of customers who were in the bank shortly prior to the robbery, and list these. Do not however, go behind the line and attempt to retrieve checks and deposit tickets to get this information. This can be done after the arrival of the police.

Each employee and customer must write down as much information as possible regarding their recollection of the bandits' description and actions as possible, without conferring with one another.

The basic thing to remember in this type of robbery is to do exactly what the bandits say (with the exception of activating the alarm at the start) and to not try to play hero.

No discussion of the bank robbery procedures is complete without the question of what to do if the shooting starts. In any robbery situation in which guns are displayed, either with the lone bandit or the gang, the remote possibility exists that the bandits, or the police, if they respond prior to the bandits departure, will become involved in shooting.

If this should happen in your bank, get down on the floor immediately and crawl under some type of cover such as a desk, table, or best of all under your teller counter. Stay as low as possible and stay under cover until all the shooting is over. Bullets are almost always fired at chest height or above, and by staying low and covered you reduce the chances of being hurt to a complete minimum.

Some robbers if cornered will try to make their escape by taking a hostage with them. This will generally be one or more bank employees. They will hold the hostage at gunpoint and take them to a waiting getaway car. If you find yourself in this position, do exactly as the robber directs. Accompany him to the car and inside the car if he so orders.

Once in the car and in motion, sit as low in the seat as possible keeping your head below window level. If at all possible, get down on the floor of the car beneath seat level and roll up in a tight ball. The bandit usually is uninterested in harming you, and only wants to use you as protection from the police. Stay in the car unless directly ordered out by the bandit, when the car stops.

Aside from these suggestions, you must use your own common sense. Try to stay as calm as possible, keep down and observe as much as possible, so that you can guide your actions for your own protection.

Remember, the police will not endanger your life just to apprehend a bank robber. Don't endanger your own life by foolish actions.

BANDIT DESCRIPTION FORM

Use separate form for each bandit and list as much descriptive data as possible, for example: Hair—*black, wavy, receding, and parted on right side.*

NAME OR NICKNAME____________________

SEX________ NATIONALITY__________ APPROX. AGE______

Height__________	Complexion__________
Weight__________	Voice__________
Build__________	Accent__________
Posture__________	Eyeglasses__________
Walk__________	Mustache__________
Hair__________	Disguise__________
Eyes__________	Hands__________
Ears__________	Gloves__________
Nose__________	Jewelry__________
Lips__________	Scars or marks__________
Teeth__________	Weapon__________

Clothing__________________________________

Other distinguishing characteristics________________

____

Method and direction of escape (include the make, model, year and license number of getaway vehicle if one was used)_____

____

____

Method of operation (what did bandit do, say, touch, etc.?)___

____

____

____

__________ _____________________________

DATE SIGNATURE

____

ADDRESS

Recommended by: THE AMERICAN BANKERS ASSOCIATION

PREVENTION

A bank is seldom prey for a criminal unless it has been thoroughly "cased." All employees should carefully observe persons loitering in or around the building and in the case of persons in cars, get license number and description of car. Employees should be discreetly wary of suspicious looking persons who seek change or open small accounts. This is a common ruse used by robbers to gain intimate knowledge of the interior of your building.

Avoid routine in the opening, closing and lunch hours of employees. Experienced burglars and robbers will carefully plan their crime and observe the movements of the various employees. If different individuals open the bank or leave for lunch at various times, and other persons close the building, such a method of operation is more likely to discourage a burglar or robber.

Inside the bank all doors leading from the customer's area of the lobby to other parts of the bank should always be locked. These include the doors leading to space behind teller's counters and rear office and rooms serving bank personnel.

Each teller should be thoroughly familiar with the "all clear" signal to be set by the bank manager, after his inspection of the bank premises each morning. This signal should be readily visible from outside the bank, and be of such nature that it is not readily apparent as a signal, to anyone except bank employees.

In the event, tellers or other bank personnel report to work and find the signal not set to indicate all clear, they should not enter the bank. They should have a prearranged point, close to the bank, but out of direct line of sight of the bank, where they can assemble.

The first person arriving at this point should be instructed to call the bank security officer, or the local police as appropriate, and advise that the all clear signal is not set, and that it is assumed there may be a hostage situation inside the bank.

BANK CURRENCY CONTROL

The amount of currency at any particular bank at any one time is subject to wide variation depending on location, season, etc. With this in mind, no universal amount can be established and this matter should be under the continuous review of the Senior Bank Officer, the Auditor, and the head teller. As a general rule, cash in a bank should not exceed 1% of deposits, unless an abnormal situation exists.

A good policy is to transport all currency and coin from the Federal Reserve or Correspondent Bank to your bank in an armored car service. While costly, it will preclude those situations of attack against an undefended bank officer transporting large sums of currency over the highway in his personal vehicle where he is open to numerous chances of attack, both planned and random.

Individual Teller Currency Procedures

The amount of currency to be kept in an individual teller's drawer should not exceed $2,500 at any one time, including "bait money." The "bait money" is to be recorded on the form provided and one copy of this form will be kept by the bank cashier.

The bait money bills should be identified by denomination, by type of bill (whether federal reserve note or silver certificate). If federal reserve note, then by federal reserve district issuing the bill, by serial number, and by series year. If the serial number ends in a star this should be indicated. Bait money should be checked, verified and restrapped with a current date strap every 30 days.

Currency not used in normal operations should be either:

1. Locked in the money portion of the vault in the individual teller's bin or
2. Locked in a safe deposit box provided for that purpose

The bank cashier or another designated officer will check the amount of cash in each cage from time to time, and should report all violations of this regulation to the bank security officer and the auditor.

BANK BURGLARY

January 1, 1975 to June 30, 1975

Commercial Banks	165
Mutual Savings Banks	4
Savings & Loan Companies	27
Credit Unions	31
Total	227

FBI BANK CRIME STATISTICS

Burglary, as the word implies, involves a stealthy attack against the banks' assets when no one is around, and the bank is closed.

Burglaries are generally committed on weekends, when the thieves have an opportunity to work undisturbed. It takes many hours to break into a well constructed vault or night depository chest. A large quantity of equipment such as cutting torches, high speed drills, core drills and thermal lances is also necessary, so it is generally not an overnight operation.

Most banks are now equipped with good vaults, safes, night depositories and burglar alarm systems, all of which have gone a long way in reducing burglaries.

The principal danger faced by bank employees in this type of crime involves the situation where an employee goes to the bank on a weekend to get something, or to do some work. If ever work is required on weekends, be sure to look over the premises from the outside first, to see if it is safe to enter.

Look to see that the standing outside and inside lights are all on and functioning. Are the window coverings open or closed as they should be? Are doors and windows securely fastened? Is there anything out of the ordinary? If so, do not enter. Call the bank manager and the police. Ask the police to come and check out the premises before entering.

Bank burglars are often local residents of shady character. They pick their target based on ease of entry and attack. Therefore, if you are aware of changes of a temporary nature which might make your bank more vulnerable, do not divulge them. A few years ago, a small rural bank was involved in moving to larger premises. The decision was made to use the old vault door in the new building. The door was moved and placed on a Friday, and the workmen put up a temporary door in the old building where the money was still located. Over the weekend, word of this fact reached a gang of burglars. This gang attacked the temporary door, broke it open and stole the bank funds.

Often information regarding a large cash shipment held temporarily in the vault will make it worth the time and effort to attack, where this would not normally be the case. If you have information of this nature, keep it to yourself.

BANK OPENING AND CLOSING PROCEDURES

The bank officer designated should be responsible for the procedures outlined below:

OPENING

1. To inspect the premises prior to entering for any signs of damage or entry
2. To inspect the interior of the office, including closets, store rooms, etc. and ascertain that no unauthorized persons are present
3. To communicate some prearranged signal to other employees that all is well and that they may enter for work
4. To open the vault as late as possible prior to banking

hours and in no instance more than 40 minutes before opening to the public

5. To check the operation of the camera if set to operate prior to opening

6. To check the operation of the telephone prior to opening

7. To inspect, on a random basis, the cash of each teller and to enforce the rules established under *Individual Teller Procedures* concerning the amount of currency in the cage

CLOSING

1. To check every area where cash and/or valuable items have been and insure that they have all been placed in the vault

2. To secure the vault as soon as possible after closing

3. To make sure that no one is in the building other than the employees

4. To make certain that the camera, if applicable, is stopped and that the lighting is in operation

5. To set the burglar alarm, lock and check all doors, etc.

KIDNAP/EXTORTION

January 1, 1975 to June 30, 1975	
Commercial Banks	163
Mutual Savings Banks	2
Savings & Loan Companies	13
Credit Unions	1
Total	179
Amount Ransom Paid	$473,150
Hostages Kidnapped	18
Injuries	2
Death	0

FBI BANK CRIME STATISTICS

Because of instances such as the brutal murder of a banker and his family in Grandin, Missouri, the banking profession has been repeatedly warned through articles in professional and commercial publications, to accept the reality of the kidnap/hostage threat to bank personnel, and to meet this threat with prior planning on an individual bank level.

The first question to be answered by each bank is "What is our exposure?" The basis for arriving at a probable answer is to look at the record.

According to the F.B.I., in a recent two year period, banks (and federally insured savings and loan associations) reported 298 instances of kidnap/extortion threats to employees of their institutions. Of these, 265 (or 99%) involved a telephone call to a bank employee, demanding money under threat. The nature of these threats were as follows:

114 callers advised there was a bomb planted (or one would be placed) in the bank or the employee's home.

102 callers advised that the bank employee or a member(s) of his family was (or would be) abducted and held hostage.

46 callers made threats so improbable or ludicrous that the employee knew the call to be a hoax immediately.

3 callers claimed to have (or an associate had) a rifle trained on the employee from outside the bank.

Of the 33 incidents not involving the use of the telephone, 4 involved letters written to the banker, 3 involved notes dropped into the night depository, and the remainder involved direct confrontation between the banker and the thief.

In 48 instances of the 298 an actual hostage situation occurred, in which 5 persons were killed and 4 injured. In cases involving the actual taking of hostages, 11 were taken from the bank premises, 33 were taken in the home, where the thief obtained entry through a ruse, and 4 were taken at home where the theif forced his way into the banker's house.

Let's look at the recipients of these 298 demands, to get the final basis for our answer. They included six board chairman, eighty-six presidents, forty-one vice presidents or assistant vice presidents, 120 branch or assistant branch managers, and forty-five lesser ranked employees (tellers or other personnel who just happened to answer the phone).

During the first six months of 1975, there were 179 instances of kidnap/extortion committed against bank officers, employees and their families alone.

Based on these statistics, the answer to our question regarding exposure seems to be this. The threat will come by telephone call to a branch or assistant branch manager. The caller will claim to have planted a bomb in the branch, or be holding a member of the victim's family hostage. The bomb threat or hostage claim will be false, and the caller will have no way to enforce his demand.

This answer would seem to solve the whole problem, but it is based only on statistics and we're dealing with actual lives. Each incident, therefore, must be judged on its own.

The day of the 'It won't happen to us" attitude is gone. The threat is here. Why? This is a new form of bank robbery with the odds in favor of the thief. His chances of detection, identification and apprehension are virtually nil. In the normal bank robbery, the bandit is restricted in location—the bank premises. He is restricted in the rank of the employee approached—the teller. He is restricted in the time allowed to commit the crime—a few minutes. He is restricted in the amount he can obtain—the teller's cash. He must show himself, thereby permitting the employee to see him, his picture to be taken, the police to be summoned, and his chances of ultimate apprehension to be greatly increased.

This new threat eliminates these risks. His location can be anywhere with a phone. His victim can be anyone from a board chairman down to the teller. His amount available can be almost any figure which he feels the bank can afford, and of most importance there is no need to show himself to anyone who can later describe and identify him. His time is not restricted. The payment of the money can be made on his terms and under conditions he sets. The statistics reveal that in 93% of the recent incidents the time for payment was set at 6 hours or less. In two-thirds of these cases, the time limit was 30 minutes or less.

The banker must know what to do if confronted with this situation. He must have a plan of action developed before the fact. The following are some of the basics of a plan developed to cope with such situations. This is only one particular way to resolve the extortion problem, by affording legal protection for bank officers.

This crime cannot be considered to fall under the Federal Bank Robbery Act (Title 18, Section 2113). Thus, any investigation by the F.B.I. has to be undertaken as a violation of the Hobbs Act, officially known as Interstate Transportation in Aid of Racketeering.

Since the Federal Bank Robbery law does not consider these crimes to be an attack against the bank, the immediate question arises of the legal implications involved in the removing of bank funds by an officer or employee to pay a ransom demand. After consultation with legal counsel, it was recommended that a bank's board of directors pass a resolution to the effect that an attack against an officer or employee (or member of their family) involving a demand for bank funds, would be considered an attack against the bank. The bank would voluntarily sustain such a loss if two conditions were met.

1. That another officer of the bank was notified of the demand and the intention to pay out the funds by the threatened employee.
2. That a law enforcement agency having jurisdiction be notified of the attack, if at all possible.

The next question involves the extent of coverage by the blanket bond for recovery of funds paid out in this type attack. Consultation with most bonding companies revealed their intention not to cover this type loss, without purchase of a separate rider. However, they would want the bank to sign a waiver of this type coverage under their present bond. You might wish to consider that the very demand for this waiver indicates that the insurer is quite possibly liable for losses of this nature. It should be noted that the A.B.A. has recommended this course of action to member banks. In addition, there have been two U.S. Circuit Court rulings in separate areas of the country that the insurers are liable under the basic blanket bond for payments on kidnap/extortion claims.

These two cases wherein the bonding company refused to pay the loss for ransom, under the Bankers Blanket Bond involving extortion were as follows:

The University National Bank of Ft. Collins, Colorado vs. Insurance Company of North America, this case was decided in favor of the bank on June 5, 1973, by the United States District Court for the District of Colorado in Denver. The bonding company did not appeal the decision.

The bank of Dade, Georgia sued the Fidelity and Deposit Company of Maryland to recover ransom payment under their blanket bond. This case was also decided in favor of the bank on December 4, 1972 by the United States District Court, Northern District of Georgia. This decision was appealed by the insurer and the decision of the District Court in favor of the bank was upheld by the Fifth Circuit Court of Appeals in August, 1973.

Consultation with local police departments and the F.B.I. have highlighted the fact that the F.B.I. should be the only law enforcement agency notified in case of a kidnap/extortion situation. In this manner, investigation can be rigidly controlled to preclude harm to the victim or his family, the ransom drop site can be covered by FBI agents in plain clothes with unmarked cars. Obviously, these men have had more experience in dealing with a potentially hazardous situation of this nature, than most local law enforcement agencies.

The last thing you want is a uniformed policeman with siren and redlight arriving at the bank or the employee's home in the middle of an actual kidnap/hostage situation.

Based on these factors, a suggested plan is detailed below.

KIDNAP/EXTORTION PROCEDURES FOR BANK OFFICERS

These procedures are predicted on the basis that the Board of Directors of your bank have passed a resolution to the effect that a kidnap/extortion demand made against any officer or employee of the bank, because of his position with the bank, will be considered as a direct attack upon the bank, and that the officer or employee is empowered to use bank funds to meet the demand, if the following circumstances are met.

1. At least one other officer of the bank is notified of the demand, and the circumstances surrounding it.
2. That the appropriate law enforcement agency, having jurisdiction is advised of the situation.

These procedures are also based on the notification of the Federal Bureau of Investigation only, as being the law enforcement agency having jurisdiction. There may be numerous situations in which this is not feasible. For example, a small bank located in a rural area may be located so far distant from immediate FBI response that notification of the Bureau would defeat the purpose. If your bank is in such a position, then the local police or sheriff would be the appropriate law enforcement agency to contact. If this is the case, it is incumbent upon your bank to immediately contact this police department (or sheriff's office) and go over with them their actions to be taken in response to such a call from you in the event of a kidnap/extortion plan.

Failure to contact them beforehand places them in a position of answering your call, if it ever comes, in the same manner as they would answer any other citizen complaint. Most local police agencies have never handled a kidnapping or extortion case, and you cannot expect them to take the correct action, unless you both have planned it in advance.

KIDNAPPING OF A BANK OFFICER AWAY FROM THE BANK PREMISES

This situation will normally arise where the officer is confronted in his home. The kidnapper will either require the officer to proceed to the bank while the kidnapper holds a member of the family hostage, or if two or more criminals are involved, one holds the family members hostage while the other accompanies the officer to the bank.

In either case, the officer must convince the kidnapper that if pre-arrangements for obtaining the money are not made, the obtaining of the money upon arrival at the bank, due to dual control procedures, could take quite some time and cause internal problems.

At this point, a call should be placed to another officer of the bank, preferably either the President or the Security Officer.

The reasons for this call are as follows:

1. Arrange for packaging of the specified amount of currency without confusion and panic
2. Assuring that bait money of proper denomination is included in the package
3. Restricting knowledge by other bank personnel that a kidnap/extortion is actually happening
4. Notifying at least one bank officer of the circumstances and intent to deliver the ransom
5. Allow notifications of the Federal Bureau of Investigation and providing them with as much information as possible. The information furnished the FBI should include the following details determined by code:
    1. who is being held hostage
    2. location of the victim(s) being held
    3. whether the criminal will accompany the officer to the bank

In order to accomplish this plan, a coded telephone call, to be followed if at all possible, is set out below. The officer receiving this call, including the President or Security Officer, should note the time the call is received, details of the conversation, time available for packaging the money, the time and circumstances regarding pickup/payment of the money.

This coded telephone call is based on a conversation of strict business formality, i.e., if the call is to Mr. Jones, he will be addressed as Mr. Thomas Jones.

SAMPLE CONVERSATION

"Hello, this is Mr. Donald Doe. I would like to speak to Mr. Thomas Jones." When the phone is answered, the victim should say, "This is Mr. Donald Doe." "Something has come up, Mr. Jones (formal)." "I would like you to have $ .... in cash, small denomination bills prepared for me." The officer receiving the call will answer, "This is a little strange, *Mr.* Doe". "Is everything alright?" At this point, the location code is inserted as follows.

"Certainly, I am alright, I am at *HOME.*" (If officer is not at home, this last sentence will be omitted thereby indicating he or his family is held somewhere else).

At this point, the time available for packaging will be inserted as follows.

"I will come to the (designated bank or branch) in about ...... minutes, please have the money ready" (or) "I will come to the (designated bank or branch) in about .... minutes and will be accompanied by a business associate." (This indicates whether one of the robbers will accompany the officer to pick up the ransom.)

The office receiving the call will now ask the officer calling "What account should I draw the money from, Mr. Doe."

At this point, the "Who is the Hostage" code will be given as follows:

1. Debit my personal account—(this means *only* the officer is being held)
2. Debit my joint account—(the officer's wife is being held)
3. Debit my expense account—(the officer and one or more family members are being held)

Upon receipt of such a call, the officer answering will take the following action:

1. Notify the FBI
2. Notify the Senior Bank Officer available
3. The manager of the designated bank or branch will be notified and the ransom money package as defined by the victim's request will be made up, being sure to include bait money of sufficient quantity and determination.
4. No personnel other than those noted above should be made aware of the situation

KIDNAP/ROBBERY

This is a situation where the criminal accomplishes his purpose by either:

1. Entering the bank during non-business hours and waiting for the bank officer (branch manager) who is to open the bank.
2. Kidnapping the officer on his way to or from work and forcing him to proceed to (or back to) the branch and open the vault.
3. Entering the officer's home and holding his family hostage while a second criminal goes directly to the branch with the officer to force him to open the vault.

In all of these cases, no demand for a specific amount of ransom is made, and the officer is neither permitted to, nor has the facilities to make a phone call as set forth in the first section of this plan.

This type crime is strictly "pot luck" wherein the criminal can only get the money to which the officer has direct access in the vault.

All bank robbers are aware of the "time lock" set up on vault doors. Most are also aware of the dual control features of money accountability in banks.

Because of these factors, the officers' first defense is to be entirely truthful with the criminal(s) in initially advising him of the time set on the time lock, and the details concerning the dual control over funds in teller safes inside the vault. Then agree to the criminals' demands, and take no action which threatens either the lives of the officer or his family.

At the time given by the robber, proceed to the branch and open the branch. If the robber(s) accompanies the manager to the branch and no one stays behind to hold members of the family hostage, the manager *should not* set the all clear signal for other employees to enter.

In accordance with existing plans, the employees, when failing to see the all clear signal, should remain outside and away from the bank, and notify the Security Officer who will dispatch the police.

While this is happening, the manager should continue to follow the robber's demands and open the vault. At this point, the crime becomes a bank robbery and will be treated and investigated as such by responding law enforcement agencies.

If the robber(s) leave a criminal accomplice behind in the manager's home to hold members of the family, the manager should proceed to the branch with the other robber(s) and prepare to open the vault. He should, on arrival, *set the all clear signal* for other employees to enter, even though there is a robber with him on the premises. This is the only way to insure the safety of family members held at home.

After other employees have arrived, there should be no attempt by bank personnel to activate the holdup alarm. The holdup alarm signals police that a robbery is occurring at the bank, it does not tell them that hostages are being held somewhere else.

From a criminal standpoint, this is the easiest type of hostage/robbery to commit and the hardest to defend against.

Officers and employees placed in this situation can only assist in the apprehension of the criminals by paying particular attention to description and identifying data of the robbers. The police cannot, of necessity, be informed until the robbery is consummated. After the robber has left the bank, notify the police and FBI *by phone.* Make them aware that your family was held hostage and that one or more of the robbers may still be at your home.

Because of the extreme danger and complexity of this type crime, it is incumbent upon bank officers to train and instruct their families in methods of defense. Be sure all family members are aware of these points because in today's criminally prone society their lives may depend on them.

1. Do not reveal any personal information to people who do not have a valid right to know. The hostage/robber has to have some knowledge of the family's make-up, living patterns and movements. He usually can get this information easily by one of the following means:

   a. conducting purported telephone, mail or face to face

surveys with the wife. For example, if in the course of such survey he found that the manager has 2 children in the local elementary school and one in the local high school, and that the wife is not employed outside the home, he now has four potential victims and he can easily approximate their daily routes, schedules and availability.

2. Do not let anyone inside your home whom you do not know. The door to door salesman and the poor fellow who ran out of gas and wants to call the garage on your phone are both potential trouble.

3. Be alert to strangers in the area.

4. Ask your neighbors to advise you concerning anyone asking questions about you or your family.

5. Positively identify visitors before opening the door to them.

6. Have adequate locking devices on all exterior opening doors, including garage door; and use them.

7. Keep your car locked when not in use and check to see there are no unauthorized passengers hiding in it before you enter.

8. If you become suspicious of a situation which could develop into this type crime, call the police, and the Bank Security Officer immediately.

THE EXTORTION DEMAND AT WORK

This situation involves a phone call to the officer, stating that unless a demand for money is met, certain things will happen. These things normally include:

1. Your home will be bombed.
2. Your bank (branch) will be bombed.
3. You or members of your family will be physically harmed.
4. Claim that a member of your family has been kidnapped and is being held.

In attempting to cope with this type crime, first consider the fact that it may be *only* a threat. Therefore, think before you act.

1. Note the time of call.

2. Keep the caller talking as long as possible. This gives you a chance to analyze his makeup such as sex, possible age, voice characteristics, accent, attitudes and response.

3. Ask appropriate detailed questions.

4. If the caller hesitates in answering any appropriate question for more than a few seconds, ask another question immediately.

a. Is this a prank?

b. Where is the bomb?

c. What time is it set to go off?

d. Is my (family member) alright?

e. What is my (family member) wearing?

f. May I talk to (family member)?

g. What do you want?

h. How do you want the money?

i. Where should the money be delivered? When?

j. How will I recognize the person to whom I should give the money?

5. Note time call was completed. Many times through the use of these questions you will expose the call as only a threat. A real extortionist will generally have the answers to these questions planned out. The phoney will stammer and be unsure or refuse to answer because he has not planned past the initial demand.

After asking these questions, if you believe the call is valid, attempt to verify some of his answers with a few quick phone calls. For example, if he claims to be holding your wife at home, *call home.* If you get no answer or a busy signal, call a neighbor and ask her to run next door on some pretense and see if your wife is alright. If your wife has gone shopping, call some stores where she may be located. If your children are purportedly involved, call the school.

If the caller has stated that there is a bomb on the bank premises make the evacuation and search for the bomb.

If as a result of this checking, you are convinced that the threat is valid, call the Security Officer or another designated officer and give them the facts concerning the threat and the directions you have received.

Following receipt of this call, the procedure should go as indicated below:

1. The Federal Bureau of Investigation will be notified.

Again do not call local police unless you have arranged with them beforehand on action to be taken

2. The President or Board chairman will be given an appraisal of the situation

3. a. if the threat is to a branch manager, the assistant manager will be advised and will prepare the ransom money package as defined by the caller, being sure to include bait money of sufficient quantity and denomination.

b. if the call is to an officer or executive at a main banking office, the head teller will prepare the ransom package, as defined by the caller, insuring that bait money of sufficient quantity and denomination is included.

4. The victim officer will follow the extortionist's instructions and deliver the ransom money. He will attempt to obtain as complete a description as possible of the criminal, his automobile and any other pertinent information

5. He will then follow the applicable procedures for bank robbery set out in the previous chapter.

EXTORTION PROCEDURES FOR TELLER PERSONNEL

Extortion threats against bank tellers and other personnel having access to working cash and funds in open vaults are showing signs of increasing.

This is a most frightening crime and has the potential for developing into a major offense to the degree of bank robbery. In fact, this crime becomes a bank robbery in which the only difference is that the robber does not physically face his victim; but uses a telephone call to accomplish his purpose.

These procedures should be followed by teller personnel of the bank in the event that they receive an extortion demand at work.

The extortion demand situation against a bank employee with ready access to working cash usually requires an immediate response and is for a sum of money to which the thief believes the victim would have ready access.

Typically this crime conforms to the following pattern. The teller receives a phone call at about the time she is to leave the bank (for lunch or at close of business). She is advised that a member of her immediate family is being held hostage and that harm will come to this family member unless the teller removes a sum of money from the teller truck (safe) and follows the caller's directions as to where to deliver the money.

The teller must act immediately. She is generally told that an accomplice is watching her actions from a point outside the bank.

The teller is warned against notifying anyone else in the bank about the call, and she is given no time in which to determine if the threat is valid.

In order to protect herself from a possible embezzlement charge, the teller must tell at least one bank employee, preferably the bank manager, of the threat and of the teller's intention to pay the money as demanded.

If the teller cannot verbally notify the bank manager, or another employee, because of time or the intimidation that she is being watched, she should follow this plan.

Take a $20.00 bill or larger and quickly write one word such as "ransom" or "robbery" on the bill. If time permits, the teller should also write any details relative to the demand. Now, concealing the bill in her hand, and while moving past another teller or the bank manager, she would drop this bill on the teller station or manager's desk.

> *NOTE:* Do not write on plain paper or a bank form. This will not be noticed, whereas any form of currency, particularly a $20.00 or larger bill will be spotted immediately.

The teller, in taking money from her teller truck for delivery, should insure that the "bait money" is included in the loot.

It is imperative that someone else in the branch know that money is being taken out to pay ransom. If no one else knows of the threat, the teller may be hard pressed to prove extortion and it will logically appear that the threat was a cover for a theft by the teller.

If the teller has been unable to verbally advise the manager or another teller, she should insure that a phone call is placed to the manager from outside the bank, after the payoff to the extortionist. This phone call should advise the manager of the details, and where the $20.00 bill containing the written warning is located, in the event it has not yet been discovered.

In the instance where the $20.00 bill warning was used, and the payoff was made immediately outside the bank, it is not feasible for the teller to hunt for a phone or travel a great distance to use one, as time for notification of police is of the essence. In this event, the teller should re-enter the bank, proceed to the nearest bank employee or customer to have him verify that she has just re-entered the bank. Have this person accompany her to find out if the $20.00 bill has been discovered. If it has not been noted, this person should accompany the teller directly to the manager and he will go with both of them to discover the bill.

The teller delivering the money should pay particular attention to the description of the person to whom she hands the money. Obtain complete data for personal identification, including make, model, and license number of the thief's car, if one is used. Note direction of escape, if thief is on foot.

The bank manager, or any other bank personnel informed of the extortion situation either verbally or by finding the $20.00 bill note, should not attempt to stop the victim from taking the money from the bank and making the payoff. They should *discreetly* follow the victim teller to assist in identification of the criminal.

After payment is made, police should be notified as in any other robbery situation, and the procedure set out in the previous chapter for bank robbery should be followed.

The best defense a teller can take against this type of crime begins at home. The extortionist has to have information of a personal nature concerning you or your family before he can make a valid threat against you, to cause you to accede to his demands. Therefore, if you will follow these suggestions, it will go a long way toward insuring that you will not be the victim of this criminal. Discuss these suggestions with family members so they are aware of them and can guide their actions accordingly.

1. Do not reveal any personal information about yourself or your family to anyone who does not have a valid right to know. Criminals posing as persons making telephone, mail or door to door surveys can obtain a great deal of information from talkative family members, such as places of employment, schools that your children attend, hours when they are at home, etc.

2. Do not let anyone inside your home who you do not know. The door to door salesman and the poor fellow whose car broke down and he wants to use your phone to call the garage are potential trouble.

3. Be alert to strangers in your area.

4. Ask your neighbors to advise you concerning anyone asking questions about you and your family.

5. If you become suspicious of circumstances which you feel may lead to this type of situation, call the security officer immediately.

Tellers should be advised that a separate kidnap plan for bank officers has been prepared. They should be told that the only part of this plan which applies to them involves the circumstances where the officer's family is held hostage at his home, and one of the robbers has come to the bank with him before opening hours to wait for the "time lock" to open on the vault.

The officer has been instructed, in this situation, to set the "all clear signal," which will mean, of course, that the teller will enter in the normal manner and find herself involved as another victim to the robbery. This is the chance which we must take to preclude any harm to the officer's family. We do *not* want the police notified until action can be taken to safeguard the family members.

If the teller finds herself in this situation, she should use the time to observe the robber at the bank. She should get a good complete description of him, as she would in any hold-up situation. At no time should a teller take action which would endanger herself, other employees, or the family held hostage. *DO NOT ACTIVATE THE HOLD-UP ALARM.*

When the bandit leaves the bank, the officer will immediately notify the FBI *by phone.* If he cannot make the call and the teller does so at his request, be sure to advise the FBI that the officer's family was held hostage and that the robbers may still be at the home, and give them the home address.

BOMB THREATS

Bomb threat calls are perpetrated by two classes of people ... those who have some real or fancied grievance against the bank, and those who like to see a lot of action for a dime. Each call must be evaluated individually, and consequently it may not be necessary to have an ironclad rule that the bank is to be evacuated in every case.

The outline which follows is divided into three areas: PLANNING STEPS ... IMMEDIATE STEPS TAKEN UPON RECEIPT OF A CALL ... AND STEPS THAT SHOULD BE TAKEN AS SOON AS POSSIBLE.

Bomb threats, in the overwhelming majority of cases, turn out to be false alarms. However, the threat to life and limb makes this a deadly serious matter, because the possibility exists that it is not a hoax.

1. PLANNING STEPS

a. A bank manager should work out a plan of action with his security people and the local police department.

b. It may be desirable to outline on small cards a sudden emergency and a slower evacuation procedure which can be distributed to key employees. Inform all employees as to what should be done in case of such an emergency.

c. In a sudden evacuation, cash drawers should be locked. Tellers should not be required to take cash to vault. The lights in departments should be left on and tellers should promptly leave the bank as soon as the lobby is cleared of customers.

d. Forethought should be given as to where the tellers may go upon leaving the bank, for shelter in foul weather.

e. A plan should be developed on how the bank is to be emptied.

f. If the bank has no public address system, employees should be educated on how to remove customers if an alarm sounds, signaling a needed evacuation.

g. Procedures should be outlined as to how the bank will be searched and which male employees will be selected for this task.

h. All employees must be trained to be on the lookout at all times for customers whose behavior is unusual. Surveillance should be maintained on customers, particularly those with packages that appear to have been wrapped at home.

i. The employee, who receives the call, is the key to initiating evacuation, and can play a role in apprehension. Employees should be given specific procedures to follow upon receipt of a call.

There are no public relations considerations when dealing with such a caller. The employee's objective should be to "needle" the anonymous caller into talking more than he had intended to. For example:

> "Look, Mister, we have dozens of these nutty phone calls every day. If you feel you've been treated unfairly by the bank,

> I'll connect you with the manager. Otherwise, kindly take your fun and games elsewhere. Would you like to speak to the manager?"

If they successfully transfer the call to a management person, they should immediately use another line to call the telephone company and have the call traced.

If the caller hangs up, the employee should immediately inform the manager of the call, giving him as much information about the caller as they can, such as... whether the voice seemed to be that of a juvenile or a mature person; hints of race or nationality; and whether drunk or sober. They should inform no one but the manager or acting manager of the call.

2. IMMEDIATE STEPS THAT SHOULD BE TAKEN UPON RECEIPT OF THE CALL

a. The employee should follow the procedure outlined above and contact the manager.

b. The police should be alerted.

c. On the basis of the instruction provided by the police, management must decide if the bank is to be evacuated.

d. If evacuation is required, an announcement similar to the one that follows should be made. "Attention please. In cooperation with the police and fire departments, we are having a test fire drill and it is necessary to immediately evacuate the bank. All customers are asked to promptly leave the bank using fire stairs and elevators." Then make the suggested following announcement:

> "Attention bank personnel. Please ask all customers to immediately leave the bank. Lock your cash drawers. Leave lights on and promptly leave the bank."

e. The manager or bank protection personnel should enlist employees to guard the bank entrances and let no one enter except police and fire personnel.

f. The manager or bank protection personnel should designate male employees to patrol floors, close fire doors, check rest rooms, evacuate stragglers, and make sure cash and records are secure.

3. STEPS THAT SHOULD BE TAKEN AS SOON AS POSSIBLE

a. The manager or bank protection personnel should seek male employees who will volunteer to search the bank; if none have been pre-selected.

b. The caller is probably in the vicinity watching the bank. If you have a camera, take several pictures of those who are watching the bank from the street.

c. Attempt to keep the incident out of all newspapers and news broadcasts.

d. Have employees meet at a designated area outside the bank.

e. Make sure employees who are late in returning to work, after the incident is resolved are not penalized in their pay.

The decision to close the bank is one for the most exacting judgment, based upon an objective evaluation. Risk is almost nil when there is reason to believe the caller is a prankster . . . but more weight must be given to the threat when it comes from an adult who gives evidence of having a grudge against the bank or who has some criminal scheme in mind.

BOMB THREAT REPORT SHEET

TIME CALL BEGAN ____________ FINISHED____________

VOICE: MALE ________ FEMALE ________ OLD ________

YOUNG ________ ACCENT ________

IS VOICE FAMILIAR?

WHO DID IT SOUND LIKE?

BACKGROUND NOISE:

TRAFFIC ____________ MUSIC ____________

VOICES ____________ PLANES ____________

TRAINS ____________ SIRENS ____________

OTHER ________________________________

If call is not recorded, or if you are unable to get other

employees to listen in, write on reverse side as much of the conversation as you can remember.

Ask the five w's: who, what, when, where, and why.

As soon as a call is terminated, call supervisor or manager, if not available, call police.

EMERGENCY PREPAREDNESS PROCEDURES

Purpose—To provide a plan for the actions of bank personnel in the event of fire, explosion, civil disturbance, bomb threat, or any other emergency situation which might require the partial or total evacuation of the bank premises.

Fire

Minor Fires—A minor fire includes such incidents as fires in ashtrays, wastebaskets or desk drawers. In the event of a minor fire in your area, do the following:

1. Go to the nearest fire alarm box and activate it or call the fire department.
2. Attempt to smother the fire, if in a wastebasket or ashtray by placing some type of covering over the container, thereby shutting off the oxygen supply to the fire.
3. If this fails, move away from the area of the fire and await arrival of fire department personnel.

Major Fires—A major fire includes any fire not immediately controllable or localized, particularly fires originating from faulty electrical equipment. In the event of a major fire in your area, do the following:

1. Pull fire alarm box or call the local fire department.
2. Evacuate the immediate area of the fire.
3. Notify the bank security officer.
4. Place bank property and assets, in vaults or cabinets as applicable, in the immediate area of the fire to protect these items from destruction. In the event that partial or total evacuation of the area or building is necessary, do this in a calm manner, in accordance with evacuation instructions contained on succeeding pages.
5. *WARNING:* If the fire is a result of faulty electrical

wiring or equipment, *DO NOT ATTEMPT TO EXTINGUISH THE FIRE WITH WATER OR SOLUTION IN FIRE EXTINGUISHERS.*

Explosion

An explosion is the violent rupturing of the physical premises due to chemical reaction. It can be caused by electrical or gas utility failure, or by man made explosive devices.

In the event of an explosion, do the following:

1. Locate nearest fire alarm box, break glass in window and pull alarm, or call the fire department.
2. Notify the bank security officer immediately.
3. Be prepared to evacuate the premises, as directed, in accordance with the evacuation plan.

CIVIL DISTURBANCE

This is a polite name for mob action resulting in group attacks on premises or personnel. These disturbances generally start as a "non-violent demonstration and end in destructive vandalism."

In the event of a civil disturbance in which an attack on the bank premises or personnel appear imminent, do the following:

1. Notify the security officer.
2. Notify the senior bank official.
3. Reduce cash to a minimum.
4. Place all vital records and excess equipment in vaults.
5. Make sure all entrance/exit doors are closed and secured. (This can be done without locking the doors, by posting personnel at the doors).
6. Remove all objects from the public lobby area, that could be used as missiles to be thrown.
7. Be prepared to place all remaining cash and equipment in vaults and evacuate premises as directed, in accordance with the evacuation plan.

BANK EVACUATION PLAN

Purpose—To provide a plan for the orderly clearing of a banks premises in the event of an emergency, to assign specific duties to personnel involved, to instruct employees in the proper securing of bank assets, proper manner of leaving the building, to provide a pattern for the proper handling of customers during an emergency.

General Information—In the event of an emergency, on a banks' premises, which includes such things as fire, explosion, bomb threat, civil disturbance, or utilities breakdown, it may be necessary to evacuate a portion, or all of the premises. Should this decision be made, your duties and responsibilities during an evacuation are set forth as follows:

Decision to Evacuate

The decision to partially or totally evacuate the banks' premises should be made by a member of management, in the following order:

1. President
2. Senior Vice President
3. Cashier

Should conditions exist where none of the above listed officers are present, the security officer shall assume the responsibility of this decision.

Notification

When the decision to declare an emergency, and evacuate a portion or all of the bank premises has been made, the member of management making this decision will immediately notify the security officer. Upon notification of the order to evacuate, the security officer will move to a central control point, such as the central switchboard or a point which utilizes centralized communications, where he will take the following action:

1. Advise the switchboard supervisor of the decision to evacuate.
2. Advise other tenants in the building if applicable of the decision.

The switchboard supervisor, when informed of the decision, will instruct the switchboard operators to ignore all incoming calls.

The switchboard supervisor will have a prepared list of phone numbers for each department head in the bank and this list will be given to the operator on duty.

The operators will phone each department head (and/or

assistant in the absence of the department head) and advise them of the emergency and the decision to evacuate the premises.

When these calls are completed the switchboard supervisor will set the switchboard for normal night operation, after which she and the operators will leave the building by pre-assigned exit routes.

Emergency Control Center

Upon the decision to evacuate the building the following members of management will immediately report to the Emergency Control Center:

1. President
2. Senior Vice President
3. Security Officer
4. Cashier

Specific Duties of Control Personnel

Members of Management—The President and Senior Vice President will direct activities regarding evacuation and make necessary decisions from the Emergency Control Center. They will be assisted by the cashier, as appropriate.

Department heads will ensure the proper securing of bank assets and property within their departments and the orderly evacuation of employees and customers from their respective departments.

The Senior Vice President will take immediate steps to insure the correct dissemination of news concerning the evacuation of the building and the reason for the declaration of emergency. He will act as a clearing house for all releases of information concerning the emergency. *NO INFORMATION SHOULD BE RELEASED BY ANY BANK PERSONNEL WITHOUT THE CONSENT OF THE SENIOR VICE PRESIDENT.*

The security officer will insure that the bank service personnel, if appropriate, are advised of the emergency and will ensure that any elevators are taken out of service and held for the use of fire and police as appropriate. He will ensure that all non-essential equipment is shut down as appropriate. He will ensure that the doors are opened in order to obtain clear paths which egress from the building. He will ensure that after the premises are evacuated all doors are reclosed and locked, consistent with emergency operations by police and fire department personnel.

The security officer will notify the operators to commence their calls to all department heads and executive officers advising them of the decision to evacuate.

The security officer will notify the local police and fire departments of the emergency and the decision to evacuate the premises.

The security officer will ensure that 15 minutes after the initial calls to department heads advising them of the evacuation, an announcement of the evacuation is made over the internal speaker system throughout the bank, if one is available.

The security officer will ensure that 5 minutes after this announcement a tour of the building is made, as appropriate by the previously designated personnel to determine that the premises have been evacuated.

Assigned bank employees preferably guards, if available, in the lobby will assist customers in the orderly evacuation of the building and will remain in the lobby area for assignment of further duties by the security officer.

> *NOTE:* Because of the possibility of panic caused by a person or persons becoming hysterical during the evacuation, assigned bank personnel are authorized to use such force as necessary to ensure the orderly departure of people from the bank premises. In the event it becomes necessary to use force against any person, a complete report concerning details will be submitted by the employee to the security officer within a reasonable period after cessation of emergency conditions.

Because of the probability of the arrival of reporters and photographers on the scene during the evacuation process, the assigned employees will advise them that all news releases will be made by the senior vice president, and proceed to give them the phone number where he can be reached. Members of news services will not be permitted to enter the premises until after complete evacuation of employees and customers, and at this time ONLY with the approval of the senior vice president.

Specific Duties of Department Heads

Upon receipt of notification to evacuate the premises, department heads are responsible to notify all of their employees of this decision. They will ensure that areas within their department such as stairwells and restrooms are checked to ensure that anyone in these areas is informed of the situation.

They will ensure that all bank assets and vital records within their departments are properly placed in vaults and other secure containers. In the event property is placed in vaults, the vaults should be locked without time setting, but with alarm systems activated.

They will ensure the orderly evacuation of their employees and customers in their department over pre-determined exit routes.

> *NOTE:* If total or partial evacuation of the premises is a result of a bomb threat, department heads and their assistants will take the following action after evacuation of employees and customers is completed.
>
> They will personally search all areas of their respective departments including restrooms, conference rooms, storage areas and closets to determine if any strange package, or article is located in any of these areas. If such an article is located, the employee will not touch the article but will immediately notify the security officer in the Emergency Control Center.

Following evacuation from the building, they will ensure that employees of their department gather in the assigned assembly area.

Use of elevators—In no circumstances are elevators to be used during an emergency situation by any bank employee for purposes of moving between floors or leaving the building. Only assigned stairwells will be used to evacuate the premises.

Personal property—Personal property should be taken only if it is in the immediate area of the employee when the decision is made and announced to evacuate the premises. If the location of the property is such that the employee will have to deviate from the exit route, it should be abandoned.

Exit routes—Each bank should have a map of the bank premises indicating the designated emergency exit route for all bank personnel and customers by section and floor. The appropriate section of the map should be placed near each exit for each specific area.

Partial clearing of the premises—All of the above procedures regarding evacuation of the premises will apply to a partial clearing of certain areas of the bank building with the following exceptions:

> Unless the switchboard area is within the area of

evacuation, the switchboard operators will remain on duty to handle calls to and from the Emergency Control Center.

Only those department heads in the affected areas will be notified to evacuate their employees and customers.

Return to premises following the emergency—Bank personnel from their vantage points outside the bank building should be able to determine when emergency equipment (police and fire vehicles) leave the area at the conclusion of the emergency.

When departure of emergency equipment is observed, department heads will obtain clearance from the Emergency Control Center for re-entry of themselves and their employees to the building.

Department heads and their employees will return to the ground floor entrance where a member of the management staff will be located to advise them regarding subsequent return to their work areas.

Drills—It is anticipated that at least one drill per year will be carried out by the bank personnel. This drill should be accomplished through coordination with thc local fire department and will be held on an announced date prior to the opening of the bank for business.

Appropriate publicity subsequent to each drill will be sought by the senior vice president as an indication of public service effort by the bank.

Employees should remember that the prime importance of these drills is to keep them informed of what to do in an emergency to protect life and property.

NOTE: "Bank customers will have no way or knowing what to do in the event of an emergency and will have to follow the advice of bank employees. Bank employees must, therefore, know what to do."

Specific Duties of the Floor Wardens

Assignment of floor wardens should be made by separate memorandum. Floor wardens will be responsible to see that the personnel working or physically located on their floor at the time the evacuation is started proceed to the correct exit and depart the floor in an orderly manner.

The floor wardens will ensure that the exit is open and clear as the personnel from that floor commence evacuation.

The floor warden will report the fact that the floor is evacuated, as soon as possible, to the security officer in the Emergency Control Room, and then proceed to join the employees of his department at the assigned assembly area.

Duties of Bank Employees

It is the responsibility of each employee to know the proper emergency exit for their work area.

Employees working in customer service areas will be expected to advise any customers located in their area at the time the evacuation is announced that "an emergency exists, please follow to the exit."

This will be done in a calm manner so as to avoid panic.

Immediately after the employee has removed himself from the building he should go to the prearranged assembly point.

After moving to these areas, employees will locate their department head and remain in proximity to him for further instructions.

Employees will make no statements to newsmen or the bystanders regarding the emergency. All such questions should be referred to the senior vice president in the Emergency Control Center.

BANK SECURITY SURVEY

CONTENTS

All footnotes refer to the indicated sections of regulation P, Bank Security Act

Yes No

BURGLARY

External Conditions

[a]1. Have local police authorities been invited to survey the premises and offer advice and recommendations with respect to improving or approving the bank's security program? .... ☐ ☐

2. Have arrangements been made for police authorities to inspect the exterior of the banking premises with reasonable frequency during nonbanking hours, particularly over weekends and holidays? .... ☐ ☐

3. Have floodlights been installed to illuminate all darkened areas surrounding the banking premises where entry might be attempted? .... ☐ ☐

4. Is exterior lighting system inspected periodically and given proper maintenance? .... ☐ ☐

5. Have local police authorities and others in the locality been asked to contact bank officials if illumination fails? .... ☐ ☐

6. Have local residents been encouraged to notify police immediately if they suspect that the bank is being "cased" or forcibly entered? .... ☐ ☐

[a]7. Are all exterior doors equipped with tamper-resistant locks? .... ☐ ☐

8. Are all doors wired with an alarm system? .... ☐ ☐

[a]9. Are all operable windows equipped with tamper-resistant locks? .... ☐ ☐

10. Are all operable windows barred? .... ☐ ☐

---

[a] Security Devices

	Yes	No
11. Are all operable windows wired with an alarm system?	☐	☐
12. Are all large plate-glass panels protected against forcible entry with an alarm system or otherwise?	☐	☐
13. Have windows in remote sections of the banking office, such as cellars, supply rooms, and washrooms, been barred and wired with an alarm system?	☐	☐
14. Are windows on upper floors that can be reached by ladders or that are accessible from adjoining structures, barred and wired with an alarm system?	☐	☐
15. If the window bars are hinged, are the hinges and pins secured so that the fastenings cannot be removed or the pins forced out?	☐	☐
16. If padlocks are used to secure bars, are they of sufficient strength to withstand the use of bolt cutters?	☐	☐
17. If bars are not hinged, are they securely set and fastenings protected against tampering?	☐	☐
18. Are bars close enough so that if one or two are bent or sprung, the opening width will not permit entrance?	☐	☐
19. Are the bars of sufficient strength and do they give the appearance of a formidable obstruction to forcible entry?	☐	☐
20. Are points of entry from fire escapes properly wired with an alarm system or otherwise protected?	☐	☐
21. Are skylights, roof hatches, manholes, bulkheads, or any other unusual openings protected against unlawful entry?	☐	☐
22. Are exhaust fans, ventilators, and air conditioners		

	Yes	No
amply protected?	☐	☐

Internal Conditions

	Yes	No
[a]1. Are banking floor and area around the vault visible from outside illuminated at night?	☐	☐
2. Are the windows clear of signs or other objects which might unnecessarily obstruct view of interior?	☐	☐
3. Are window shades or blinds adjusted to permit view of banking floor?	☐	☐
4. Are floors, walls, and ceilings wired with an alarm system as a defense against boring through?	☐	☐
5. If not, has an electronic or other available intrusion detection device designed to protect against burglars been installed?	☐	☐
6. Are all entrances to the banking office from basement, elevators, or stairs equipped with strong and efficient locks and wired with an alarm system?	☐	☐
7. Is the main vault alarm system equipped with a heat-sensing and/or smoke-sensing device?	☐	☐
[b]8. Is someone responsible for ascertaining that all security devices are turned on and operating during the periods in which such devices are intended to be used?	☐	☐
[b]9. Is someone designated to be responsible to assure that all valuables, including currency, coin, securities, etc., have been put away in a locked vault or safe during non-banking hours?	☐	☐

[b]10. Is someone responsible to ensure that no unauthor-

[a] Security Devices
[b] Security Procedures

Yes No

ized persons are present in the banking office after closing hours? . . . . ☐ ☐

[b]11. Is someone responsible for ascertaining that the vault, safe, doors, and windows are securely locked after closing hours? . . . . ☐ ☐

12. Is a night watchman employed by the bank? . . . . ☐ ☐

13. Is the investigation sign of the FBI prominently displayed? . . . . ☐ ☐

Alarms (*also see section under Holdup*)

[a]1. Is an audible and/or a silent burglar alarm system installed in the banking office? . . . . ☐ ☐

[a]2. If an audible alarm system, is the alarm connected with a loud-sounding gong, bell, or other device outside of building? . . . . ☐ ☐

3. Can the sounding device be heard over all noises in the vicinity and for a distance of at least 500 feet outside the banking office? . . . . ☐ ☐

[c]4. If a silent alarm system, is it connected to a central signal station or a local police station? . . . . ☐ ☐

[c]5. If not, is it connected with a source that can relay a trouble signal to police? . . . . ☐ ☐

6. Is the audible and/or silent alarm system a closed circuit system? . . . . ☐ ☐

7. If not, is the entire alarm system safeguarded against tampering which would render it ineffective? . . . . ☐ ☐

---

[a] Security Devices
[b] Security Procedures
[c] Appendix A

	Yes	No
[b]8. Is the alarm system tested periodically to assure it is in good working order?	☐	☐
[b]9. Is the alarm system inspected and serviced under the terms of a maintenance contract with the manufacturer?	☐	☐
[b]10. Is a record kept of such inspections, testings, and servicing?	☐	☐
[c]11. In the absence of an alarm system, is there any other appropriate device to assist in promptly notifying law enforcement officers of a burglary?	☐	☐
[c]12. Is the alarm system safeguarded against accidental transmission?	☐	☐
[c]13. Is the alarm system equipped with a visual and audible signal to indicate malfunctioning of or tampering with the system?	☐	☐
[c]14. Is the alarm system equipped with an independent source of power to assure continuous reliable operation in the event of a power failure?	☐	☐

Vaults and Safes (*also see section under Holdup*)

	Yes	No
[c]1. Is vault protected by timelock?	☐	☐
[c]2. Is vault equipped with a relocking device?	☐	☐
[c]3. Is vault protected by an alarm system?	☐	☐
[c]4. Is the alarm installation complete, protecting the vault door, all walls, floor and ceiling?	☐	☐
5. Is the alarm system a Grade A Complete System listed by Underwriters' Laboratories, Inc.?	☐	☐

---

[b] Security Procedures
[c] Appendix A

Yes No

6. Is the vault protected with a tear gas system? .... ☐ ☐

7. Are safe deposit boxes kept in the main vault or a separate vault offering equal protection? .... ☐ ☐

8. Are vault combinations under dual control? .... ☐ ☐

[c]9. Is the vault well constructed of drill and torch-resistant materials? .... ☐ ☐

Vault Classification

10. If the banking office is equipped with a safe not stored in a vault, is the safe of heavy construction which is drill- and torch-resistant? .... ☐ ☐

[c]11. Are all safes equipped with combination locks and with relocking devices? .... ☐ ☐

The A.B.A. Insurance and Protective Committee, upon request, will provide the construction requirements for safe and vault classifications of insurance underwriters. The highest vault classification listed is No. 10R, the lowest No. 1.

Night Depositories

1. Is the night depository safe constructed to meet the B(2) classification of burglary insurance underwriters? ..... ☐ ☐

A B(2) safe requires (a) a combination locked round or screw solid steel door at least 1½ inches thick and (b) a body of solid steel at least 1 inch thick.

[c]2. Is the chute leading from the head and the envelope slot (if any) to the safe constructed of solid steel 1 inch thick or ¼-inch thick encased in 6 inches of reinforced concrete? . ... ☐ ☐

---

[c] Appendix A

Yes No

[c]3. Are the head to the chute on exterior of bank and the interior of the chute constructed to prevent "fishing" or trapping of deposits? . . . . ☐ ☐

4. Is the envelope slot ½-inch by 5 inches or less? . . . . . ☐ ☐

5. Have depositors been cautioned against overloading pouches and envelopes which might clog the head or chute and facilitate theft? . . . . ☐ ☐

[c]6. Is the night depository protected by an alarm system? . . . . ☐ ☐

7. The following questions relate to additional safeguards:

(a) Has the bank a proper agreement with depositors providing for verification of each deposit on the next banking day? . . . . ☐ ☐

(b) If each depositor does not receipt for and open his own pouch or packet, is each pouch or packet opened and the contents examined and verified by at least two bank employees? . . . . ☐ ☐

(c) Are users of the night depository required to mail or deposit in bank's mail slot a duplicate deposit slip for each deposit? . . . . ☐ ☐

(d) Is the total amount of the bank's blanket bond and excess burglary and robbery insurance on the night depository safe sufficient to cover maximum total deposits made during holidays and weekends when the bank is closed two or more days? . . . . ☐ ☐

HOLDUP

Tellers Area

1. Is there sufficient protection in front of tellers

[c] Appendix A

Yes No

counters to deter bandits from leaping over them? .... ☐ ☐

2. Are tellers counters designed so that alarm actuators, cash, and other valuables are not exposed to public view? .... ☐ ☐

3. Are doors or gates to tellers area locked or otherwise protected against unauthorized admittance? .... ☐ ☐

[b]4. Is each teller's cash (including drive-in and walk-up tellers) kept to a reasonable minimum at all times? .... ☐ ☐

[b]5. Is "decoy" or "bait" money placed in each teller's cash drawer and instructions given as to its use, and are proper records maintained as to the description of such decoy currency? .... ☐ ☐

[c]6. Are drive-in or walk-up banking facilities of bullet-resistant construction? .... ☐ ☐

7. Are these facilities protected by alarm system? ..... ☐ ☐

8. Can personnel in a drive-in or walk-up facility safely communicate with customers and the banking office providing the facility? .... ☐ ☐

[b]9. Is adequate protection given to bank funds in transit to and from all tellers stations, including drive-in and walk-up facilities, and to and from the vault or other protected place? .... ☐ ☐

Guards and Floormen

1. Does the bank employ guards or floormen? .... ☐ ☐

2. When armed, are they proficient in the use of firearms? .... ☐ ☐

---

[b] Security Procedures
[c] Appendix A

	Yes	No
3. Is there a signal system within the banking office to alert officers, guards, or floormen of a holdup in progress?..	☐	☐
4. Are guards or floormen instructed to avail themselves of police assistance whenever time and circumstances permit?	☐	☐
5. Are guards or floormen stationed where they can observe as much of the banking floor as possible?	☐	☐
6. Is it a bank policy that guards are not to leave their posts to perform incidental duties, such as trivial errands inside or outside the banking office?	☐	☐
7. Are guards instructed to approach anyone arousing suspicion and ask, "May I help you?"	☐	☐
8. When it is necessary for a guard to be absent from the banking office for reasons of illness, vacation, luncheon periods, etc., is a qualified employee available to assume his duties?	☐	☐

Alarms

Audible alarms with loud-sounding gongs or sirens and central station alarms are recognized by insurance underwriters as effective protection against burglary. Audible alarms, however, are not recognized as effective protection against holdup. Generally, burglary and holdup alarms operate through the same system. In addition to the questions on alarms under Burglary, the following questions should be answered with respect to Holdup:

[a]1. Is a silent holdup alarm or other appropriate device installed in the banking office?	☐	☐

[c]2. Is the silent alarm connected to a central signal

[a] Security Devices
[c] Appendix A

Yes No

station or a local police station? . . . . ☐ ☐

[c]3. If not, is it connected with a source that can relay a trouble signal to police? . . . . ☐ ☐

4. If the banking office is equipped with both a loud-sounding alarm and a silent alarm, is the audible alarm disconnected during banking hours? . . . . ☐ ☐

[c]5. Are the silent alarm actuators conveniently placed in each teller's station and other areas where personnel might be approached by a bandit? . . . . ☐ ☐

6. Are alarm actuators installed in vaults, washrooms, and other places where employees could be confined by bandits? . . . . ☐ ☐

7. Is there an alarm actuator at a desk purposely situated to give a maximum view of the banking floor? . . . . . . ☐ ☐

8. Is a bank officer, an employee, or a guard assigned to this desk at all times? . . . . ☐ ☐

Surveillance Systems

[c]1. Is surveillance system capable of reproducing images of persons in the banking office with sufficient clarity to facilitate, through enlargements, the identification of robbers or suspicious persons? . . . . ☐ ☐

[c]2. If a camera system, are the cameras capable of taking at least 1 picture every 2 seconds and using film of at least 16 mm in amount sufficient to operate for not less than 3 minutes continuously? . . . . ☐ ☐

[c]3. Is system capable of activation by initiating devices at or in close proximity to each teller's station? . . . . ☐ ☐

---

[c] Appendix A

Yes No

[c]4. Does surveillance system cover all teller positions and each exit? . . . . ☐ ☐

5. Are cameras mounted out of reach? . . . . ☐ ☐

[c]6. Are cameras enclosed in tamper-proof housing and reasonably silent in operation? . . . . ☐ ☐

[c]7. Is surveillance system serviced, inspected, and tested at reasonable intervals for proper operation, including aiming, focusing, and the loading of film or tape? . . . . ☐ ☐

[c]8. Is someone responsible for seeing that surveillance system, if automatic and continuous, is turned on and operating during periods when such device is intended to be in use? . . . . ☐ ☐

9. Are decals or other signs posted warning that banking office is protected by cameras? . . . . ☐ ☐

Vaults and Safes

In addition to the questions on vaults under Burglary, the following questions should be answered with respect to Holdup:

1. Is signaling equipment, such as an alarm, buzzer or telephone, installed in the vault to facilitate release of any person locked inside? . . . . ☐ ☐

2. Is each vault equipped with an emergency vault ventilator listed by Underwriters' Laboratories, Inc.? . . . . ☐ ☐

[b]3. Is opening of the vault delayed to the latest practical time before business hours? . . . . ☐ ☐

[b]4. Is the vault closed as soon as practical after the closing hour? . . . . ☐ ☐

---

[b]Security Procedures
[c]Appendix A

Yes No

5. Is there a safe at each teller's station or within the vault equipped with a delayed action timelock in which to keep excess cash? . . . . ☐ ☐

6. If not, is there a locked compartment in which a teller can place excess cash during the working day? . . . . ☐ ☐

[b]7. Is a reasonable amount of "decoy" or "bait" money maintained in the safe(s) for excess cash? . . . . ☐ ☐

Opening Hours

[b]1. Before the banking office is opened each day, does a guard or other person inspect the exterior of the premises for signs of forcible entry to avoid ambush from within? . . . . ☐ ☐

[b]2. Does the guard or other person then inspect the interior of the banking premises before admitting other personnel? . . . . ☐ ☐

[b]3. Does a guard or other designated person admit employees in the morning? . . . . ☐ ☐

[b]4. Is entry refused to unknown persons? . . . . ☐ ☐

[b]5. Is a prearranged signal transmitted to arriving personnel to confirm that all is well before they enter the banking office? . . . . ☐ ☐

6. Is there a prearranged signal whereby arriving officers and employees accompanied by strangers, can indicate if they are under duress? . . . . ☐ ☐

7. Are officers and employees instructed to be on the lookout for suspicious persons who may be "casing" the bank? . . . . ☐ ☐

8. Have local police been requested to be present at the

---

[b] Security Procedures

Yes No

bank for a reasonable time prior to and following its opening? . . . . ☐ ☐

Luncheon Hours

1. Are luncheon hours staggered so that as many employees as possible will be on duty? . . . . ☐ ☐

2. Are employees instructed to be especially alert during luncheon hours when the size of the staff is reduced? . . . . ☐ ☐

Closing Hours

[b]1. Are employees instructed to place currency, coin, securities, and other valuables in vault at earliest possible moment? . . . . ☐ ☐

2. Have local police been requested to be present at the banking office for a reasonable time prior to and following its closing? . . . . ☐ ☐

3. Are all employees instructed to leave premises at a designated exit? . . . . ☐ ☐

4. Is a guard, floorman or other employee stationed at the designated exit? . . . . ☐ ☐

5. Are officers and employees instructed to be on the lookout as they leave for suspicious persons who may be "casing" the bank? . . . . ☐ ☐

Personnel Training

[b]1. Are employees trained and conditioned to anticipate the possibility of a holdup? . . . . ☐ ☐

[b]2. Does their training include the proper use and activation of security devices? . . . . ☐ ☐

---

[b] Security Procedures

Yes No

[b]3. Are your employees periodically retrained in their responsibilities under the bank's security program? . . . . ☐ ☐

[d]4. Does the training program include the following instructions? . . . . ☐ ☐

During Holdup

(a) Try to remain as calm as possible and be observant.

(b) Concentrate on the description of the bandit nearest you.

(c) Note whether bandit is wearing a mask or other disguise, also whether he is armed.

(d) Note names by which bandits refer to one another.

(e) Estimate their ages and weights and compare their heights with your own or a convenient object.

(f) Observe any peculiarities in their physical appearance, speech, dress, or movements.

(g) Note whether they hold weapons in right or left hands.

(h) Follow the instructions of armed bandits.

(i) If a note is passed, retain the note unless instructed to return it.

(j) Although a bandit does not display a weapon, consider the safety of bank personnel and customers before attempting to stall him or otherwise thwart the attack.

(k) Without jeopardizing personal safety, activate silent alarm or other device and surveillance system at earliest practical moment.

(l) Hand out as little cash as possible and include "decoy" or "bait" money in the loot.

(m) Avoid actions that might increase danger to self or to others.

After Holdup

(a) Immediately alert other bank personnel to the situation.

---

[b] Security Procedures

[d] Appendix B

Yes No

(b) Local police and the FBI should be quickly notified.

(c) If possible, follow bandits at a safe distance to determine their means and direction of escape.

(d) Obtain description and license number of getaway car, also descriptions of any accomplices.

(e) Preserve crime scene from destruction of fingerprints and other evidence until police arrive.

(f) Write down descriptions of bandits, getaway car, and other details of holdup. (Forms may be distributed to employees for this purpose.)

(g) Do not discuss details of holdup with anyone except police authorities or designated bank officials.

(h) Refer inquiries by the press to a designated bank official or police authorities.

(i) Details of holdup should be promptly reported to appropriate Federal and state agencies, bonding companies, and The American Bankers Association.

(j) If robber leaves before police arrive, assure that a designated officer or employee waits outside the banking premises, if it is safe to do so, to inform police when they arrive that the robber has left.

(k) Attempt to determine the names and addresses of other witnesses to the robbery or the escape, and request them to record their oservations or to assist a designated officer or other employee in recording their observations.

Firearms

1. Does the bank keep a record of the make, model, caliber, and serial number of each firearm? . . . . ☐ ☐

2. Are precautions taken to guard against theft or unauthorized removal? . . . . ☐ ☐

3. Are firearms cleaned and serviced periodically? . . . . . ☐ ☐

4. If firearms are cleaned or serviced by an outsider, is the serial number on each firearm checked when they are returned? . . . . ☐ ☐

Yes No

5. Is ammunition replaced within period recommended by manufacturer? .... ☐ ☐

6. Have licenses been obtained for firearms where required by state laws? .... ☐ ☐

7. Are all personnel who are equipped with firearms required to be proficient in the care, handling, and use of such weapons? .... ☐ ☐

SNEAK THEFT

1. Is a minimum amount of coin and currency taken from the vault or timelocked safe to commence each day's business? .... ☐ ☐

2. Are all incoming deliveries of cash and securities made to a designated officer or employee within the confines of a teller's station or other appropriate location and promptly recorded? .... ☐ ☐

3. Is surplus cash accumulated during business hours placed in timelocked safe? .... ☐ ☐

4. Are all securities other than as needed kept in a specified securities vault or in a timelocked safe in the main vault? .... ☐ ☐

5. Is all currency in tellers area, particularly the head teller's station, a sufficient distance from customers to avoid a quick snatch of the funds? .... ☐ ☐

6. Are all unissued forms such as money orders, travelers checks, bonds and similar instruments, afforded adequate protection against sneak theft? .... ☐ ☐

7. Are tellers instructed to take appropriate measures to safeguard valuables whenever necessary to leave their stations? .... ☐ ☐

Yes No

8. Are tellers cautioned against being distracted by telephone calls or other methods used by persons contemplating a sneak theft? . . . . ☐ ☐

DETERMINING APPROPRIATENESS OF SECURITY DEVICES

[a]1. Has your bank sought the advice of law enforcement authorities in determining the appropriateness of security devices and recorded the name and rank of the law enforcement officer consulted? . . . . ☐ ☐

2. Is the bank aware of the incidence of crimes against financial institutions in the area in which the banking office is located? . . . . ☐ ☐

3. Is the bank aware of the distance from the nearest responsible law enforcement officers and the time required for such officers ordinarily to arrive at the banking office? . . . ☐ ☐

4. Has the bank taken into consideration the amount of currency or other valuables exposed to robbery, burglary, or larceny? . . . . ☐ ☐

5. Has your bank considered the Implementation provision under Security Devices in the regulations? . . . . ☐ ☐

6. If your bank has decided not to install devices at least equivalent to the standards described in the regulations, is a statement of the reasons for such decision preserved in your bank's record as required under the implementation provision? . . . . ☐ ☐

---

[a] Security Devices

Index